FROM
ROCK BOTTOM
TO ROCK SOLID

SCOTT J. PRENDERGAST

FROM
ROCK BOTTOM
TO ROCK SOLID

LEARNING TO NAVIGATE LIFE
THROUGH THE LENS OF HOPE

PALMETTO
P U B L I S H I N G
Charleston, SC
www.PalmettoPublishing.com

Paperback ISBN: 979-8-8229-3466-5
eBook ISBN: 979-8-8229-3467-2

To Jesus Christ of Nazareth. You are the true Emergency Joy in my life. Thanks for pulling me out of my despair and showing me true life! To my beautiful wife, Rosa. Thank you for always supporting me unconditionally. You're everything I could have ever dreamed of in a woman and more. I love you! To Mom, Dad, Victoria, and Angela. Thanks for always being in my corner since day one and always believing in me!

TABLE OF CONTENTS

INTRODUCTION

Throughout my life I've consistently found myself gravitating to the in-between. Not too hot, not too cold. Like Goldilocks, I've always been searching for that just-right place to be. Unfortunately, in today's society there seems to be less and less middle ground, as everyday life has become a barren wasteland of all or nothing. Either you're this, or you're that, no in-between. Perhaps that's why everyone is so angry all the time: Where's the bowl of porridge that's just right? The same can be said for the self-help book market. So many books are frivolous and salesy, with catchy titles meant to dazzle the eye, yet filled with absolutely useless content that leaves you feeling swindled upon reading it. On the other end of the spectrum, you have these brilliant scholarly minds writing books that boost their egos and prove their well-crafted theses and dissertations to be valid, but you need fifteen different degrees under your belt to understand what in the world they're talking about.

Once again, upon seeing this market of self-help books, I find myself longing for the middle ground. A book that's not some cheap money-making title that's a precursor for a paid course, but at the same time a book that doesn't require me to have my PhD to understand its content.

This longing for middle ground is exactly why I wrote this book you're about to read. I wanted to write something for the everyday person who's struggling with the everyday obstacles we all face in life. I wanted to help inspire people from all backgrounds and ages with a book that anyone can understand and relate to. A book that teaches people how to rediscover their hidden resilience that has been buried for years, a book that brings forth hope and inspires the reader to take action. I want this book to be something that people can hold on to during the rocky times in life, and something that brings validation and comfort to whatever struggle is faced. What I ended up writing is a collection of my own life experiences, combined with legitimate strategies that I know will help you overcome whatever obstacles life throws your way and help you to navigate your life through the lens of hope. I hope you enjoy it. Welcome to the middle ground, Goldilocks. Enjoy the bowl of porridge that's just right!

CHAPTER ONE

THE CORE BELIEF CONUNDRUM

Your core values are the deeply held beliefs
that authentically describe your soul.
—John C. Maxwell

"If you believe you can, you will." These are the words that echoed through my head as I stepped onto Temple University's campus as a freshman in 2015. I couldn't quite remember where I had heard that old quote, but for some reason it always seemed to resurface in moments when I was in need of a reminder. Although I'd never been a fan of the whole "Pinterest quote" thing, the idea of believing I could do something, followed by accomplishing it, seemed extremely attractive. Especially because I was looking for any reason to believe in myself as I started college. Everyone said college was going to be a "clean slate," a "new beginning," "a chance to start over," and that all sounded great to me, but more than anything I just wanted to believe in myself for the first time.

I wanted to change my narrative and live a life of confidence, instead of being obedient to the voices of self-doubt that routinely squashed my dreams. If you want to talk about something I had in abundance, self-doubt would top that list! Ever since I could remember, I always doubted myself, whether it was in school, talking with girls, playing sports, you name it. Confidence was something that seemed to elude me for most of my life, and that manifested into an internal core belief that I would never be enough. I carried that core belief onto Temple University's campus with me, eager to part ways with it, yet unsure of how to do so.

As move-in day came and went, I found myself looking for any opportunity to prove to myself that I could be confident. I remember walking down the hallways, knocking on every single dorm room introducing myself to complete strangers and their parents, who most likely thought I was an RA checking up on their move in. Sure enough, with each door opened, another person was added to my newfound posse. As a result, I found myself building that ever-so-elusive confidence more and more. At one point I had amassed a group of about twenty-five kids (many who surely lacked confidence as well) going with me from door to door looking to get started on the college experience as soon as possible. None of us knew what the future held, but all of us wanted to start fresh, and I couldn't have asked for a better way to start doing just that. I figured even if I wasn't confident at all, no one else had to know that, so why not going around pretending to be what I wanted to be? For a wide-eyed freshman that seemed pretty great, but in the back of my mind I wondered how long I could keep the charade up.

If you are reading this, I would assume you're ready for me to tell you from that day on, I never looked back, and my life was filled with confidence that would last my entire college career. Well, friends, this isn't a fairy-tale book; in fact, it's the opposite: a book about the realities of the mental obstacles that hold us all back in life and how to work through them. The fact is, confidence wasn't found consistently in my life until after college was over, so the fairy tale never really got a chance to blossom during those freshman college days.

Speaking of fairy tales, college was far from that, which surprised me, because as I mentioned, I assumed college was going to be the magic formula that made all my problems disappear.

As freshman year turned into sophomore year, then junior year turned to senior year, I consistently found myself stuck in between two beliefs. The first was that I would never be enough for anything or anyone, but the second was that I could achieve anything I set my mind to. It was strange because I always found myself balancing both these beliefs, with neither one ever fully tipping the scales. Nevertheless, it seemed that anytime I had confidence, those old negative core beliefs would sweep it away as if it'd never been there. Oddly enough though, as soon as I started falling into that familiar self-pity, the belief that I could do anything I set my mind to started to rise up in me and inject me with the confidence necessary to keep moving forward.

For years I struggled with the duality of these two core beliefs, and, admittedly, I assumed I would always struggle with the yin and yang of my negative and positive views of myself, unable to fully shed that insecure skin that cloaked me for so many years. Key word here is *assumed*... because it wasn't until I stopped assuming and starting assessing that I saw real change occur in myself from the inside out. The rest of this chapter will discuss how I was able to do that and the steps that you can take to break out of the negative core beliefs that plague your own mind.

What is a core belief? That's a good question, and let's address that before anything else. A core belief is a deeply held assumption about ourselves, the world, and others. This might not sound like much, but these beliefs are deeply embedded in our thinking patterns, and they greatly shape our reality and behaviors. Like most things, there are two sides to core beliefs. We have positive core beliefs such as the following: "I am enough exactly the way I am"; "Difficulties I face will only make me stronger"; "If I set my mind to something, I can achieve anything." Then we have our good old negative core beliefs such as these: "No matter what I do, no one will like me"; "I'll never be successful because I'm stupid"; "I mess up everything good in my life."

I'm sure that after you look at these examples, there is at least one belief there that you can identify with at some point in your life, or that you're dealing with now. The argument could certainly be made that core beliefs are the primary reason we act the way we act and behave the way we do on a daily basis. Our core beliefs serve as a lens that we see every life experience and situation through. Think of it like a filter you would put on an Instagram post. That filter doesn't change the actual picture itself, but it skews what you see, portraying something that might not actually be true or making it appear different than the reality. That's the amazing, yet scary, thing about these beliefs that we hold; they have such great power to change our lives, for better or worse.

But how is it that a tiny little belief, something that we can't even see, can have that much of a say in what we do and who we become? The list is far and wide, but let's start with one word: childhood. Many of the core beliefs that we carry around today as adults stem from our younger, more impressionable years. The reasoning behind this has to do with the fact that our brain is still developing during these years, and when we experience a certain event or situation, it leaves an impression on us. Typically, the breakdown is as follows:

A particular experience is had in youth.

Then,

unhelpful conclusions and assumptions are made.

Life is then lived assuming these conclusions that were made in childhood were true.

Then an impactful incident later in life occurs, serving as evidence to those negative conclusions that were made as a youth.

Followed by automatic negative self-talk and rumination.

Followed by symptoms of a mental health challenge.

The interesting thing about this cycle is that it's so difficult to identify, because we get caught up in what I like to call "autopilot mode." Autopilot mode is when those negative thoughts such as "I'll never be enough" or "I can never do anything right" start popping up in our heads without us being conscious about it. The official name for this autopilot mode is *automatic negative self-talk*, and it's quite the bully if I've ever known one. This automatic negative self-talk is one of, if not the main contributing factor in developing negative core beliefs about ourselves, whether at a young age or even as full-grown adults.

What makes negative self-talk so dangerous is that it plays off our previous experiences. Experiences that we've viewed as traumatic or hurtful in some type of way go hand in hand with negative self-talk. They feed off each other, hence creating one-third of the cycle aforementioned. I can recall numerous situations throughout my life where I fell victim to this cycle, but the one that rises to the top is a story of me as an eight-year-old student.

I remember back in elementary school, I had a teacher who would yell and scream at students for even the slightest imperfections. It's hard to imagine eight-year-olds being anywhere close to perfection, but her teaching style demanded it! One day I was creating a craft for our class party before we went on holiday break, and apparently, I didn't cut the paper to the exact specifications required by this teacher's classroom dictatorship. As a result, I received a royal tongue-lashing about the inability to follow directions correctly and was told to begin the project again, while my nervous classmates stared at me in pure terror. Even as a strong-willed eight-year-old boy, I gave in to the overwhelming desire to tear up, and proceeded to half-heartedly attempt to start the project over again while everyone else enjoyed recess time.

Now this seems like a pretty ordinary story that most of us can relate to in some way. It's not uncommon to have an experience like this; something similar has happened to many of us. In my case, it was the first time that I had ever been yelled at by a teacher. As a result of this experience, the view I had of myself changed. I started to believe that I could never follow directions correctly, and I saw self-doubt begin to manifest when faced with classroom assignments, sporting events, and pretty much everything. I had such a fear of being humiliated and embarrassed that I would routinely ask others if I was doing even the most basic tasks correctly, such as raising my hand to go to the bathroom. This experience, and others like it, led to a core belief that I wasn't able to do anything right, and I carried this belief around with me for years.

Now to be clear, this one incident is not solely to blame for this core belief that I had; as mentioned before, there is a cycle that takes place. However, it was one of many experiences that served as evidence for myself to use when negative self-talk started talking trash to me. Every time I started to hear that familiar voice of self-doubt, and when I tried to dismiss it, that voice would point back to experiences, (such as the one with my third-grade teacher) as proof that I couldn't do anything right.

To give you a more specific idea of this process, I want you to walk with me here for a moment. Imagine every day as you leave your home there is this person who comments on how you look. Some days they compliment you, telling you how beautiful or handsome you are and all the amazing things you're going to do throughout the day. However, most days they point out all the things wrong with you and who you are as a person. They hyperfocus on your flaws and tell you all the reasons why you'll never succeed; they bring up all the bad experiences you've had in the past and remind you of the nasty things people have said and done to you over the years. Well, my friends, that person isn't waiting outside your home. In fact, that person isn't even a person at all. That "person" is within you, and its real name is negative self-talk.

If we spend enough time listening to it and agreeing with it, then it will begin to change our core beliefs entirely. But let's take a deeper look at this negative self-talk so we can better understand the impact it has on our core beliefs. For the sake of ease, let's call this bully Todd (negative self-talk). Like any bully, it didn't come to power overnight; it gained a reputation over the years through experiences. Todd is made up of all the insecurities, trauma, and letdowns from your past, and it takes the feelings and emotions associated with all those experiences and begins to form them into a weapon to be used against yourself. Todd thrives on spewing hurtful comments as you look at yourself in the mirror and loves to play the role of historian—bringing up those past hurtful experiences. Like any bully, Todd gains strength and power every time you feed into what's being said.

So how do we fight back against this menacing Todd? That's a good question, and we'll most certainly get to that. However, before we can defeat Todd, we have to learn to identify when Todd is beginning to play his usual games and antics. So how do we identify Todd? I want you to try something. Think back to when you woke up today; what was the first thing Todd said to you? (Just a reminder that "Todd" is negative self-talk.) Did you agree with what Todd said? Did you do anything to fight back and challenge that thought? Or maybe you just accepted it as a "truth" and allowed this thought to get comfortable and put down roots within your conscious thinking.

Be honest with yourself and think about which answer best describes how you handled that internal criticism this morning. Trust me—it's okay if you let it affect you and accepted that negativity as truth. I've been there too many times myself to even count! But if you are able to at least acknowledge that, you're on the right path, because now you're aware of it. Doesn't sound like much, right? But believe me, it is! Once you become aware of Todd, his power is greatly diminished. The element of sneaking around, whispering little thoughts of inferiority, hopelessness, and self-pity without being identified, is his strongest tactic.

Now that you've become aware of Todd, you have to make sure you can continue to identify him so you don't succumb to that same old negative cycle. I've found one of the simplest, yet best ways to stay aware of Todd throughout the day is by making a list of the attacks. This list isn't a wish list to Santa Claus; it's more of an eye-opening list for you to see how often Todd spews lies to you. By simply writing down the times you see yourself falling victim to negative self-talk, you shine a light on the pattern you've been stuck in.

Many times, when we get stuck in these negative thought patterns fueled by negative self-talk, we fall into thought distortions such as all-or-nothing thinking. This is when we see only two outcomes: it's all going to be amazing, or it's all going to be terrible, no in between. Another common thought distortion is called *catastrophizing*. This is when we view a situation as—you guessed it—catastrophic, such as, "If I don't pass this test, I'll surely fail out of school and become homeless for the rest of my life."

I think we can see how falling into thought distortions like this are detrimental to us in numerous ways. In order to overcome that negative thinking and the patterns associated with it, we must become self-aware of these types of thoughts. One of the best ways to do that is to get these thoughts down on paper as aforementioned. When we make our list throughout the day of our thoughts and feelings (which are very real in the moment), and after analyzing them later, we can see how they lean toward the irrational side of thinking. The process of taking time to separate and actively write down our thoughts pulls us away from that anxious loop and grounds us toward a more levelheaded space.

This is why learning to identify these attacks from Todd is so crucial: so that we can see these anxious and self-detrimental thoughts for what they are—oftentimes irrational and untrue assumptions. The great thing about this process is that writing down our thoughts leads to analyzing and, ultimately, questioning our thoughts. This helps us come one step closer to being able to replace those negative thoughts from Todd and, instead, fill our minds with thoughts that are productive, which ultimately puts us on the path to changing our core beliefs.

Now I would say the most important ingredient that needs to be added to this whole equation is time. This ingredient isn't sexy; it's not trendy; it's not something you post about on your socials, but it's the most essential part of changing our core beliefs from negative to positive. We can identify our negative thoughts all day long, and we can even practice replacing them, but if we don't give this process time, it will never stick. When it comes to working through core beliefs, I like to think of time as the keys to the car. We have our strategies and techniques; that's all the fancy features the car has, like the Bluetooth, the built-in navigation system, the twenty-four-inch chrome wheels. But without the keys, the car is nothing more than something to stare at. What good is it if the engine can't be started?

Without giving ourselves time, we cannot expect to change years of negative beliefs about ourselves. This isn't a process that changes over two days, two weeks, or even two months. It's a process that requires persistence, adjustment, and time to cultivate new core beliefs. I've always struggled explaining this to people I work with because everyone wants results immediately. I can't tell you how many times I've heard, "Scott, I've been practicing positive self-talk for nine days straight and it hasn't changed anything."

With respect, are you serious?

We need to understand that the brain is a muscle just like any other, and muscle memory is formed through repetition. Just like you wouldn't expect six-pack abs after two workouts, you can't expect to adopt an entirely new way of thinking after two weeks. For some this can be discouraging, since many are seeking that instant gratification adored by this world, and a process that doesn't offer that seems archaic to some. However, make no mistake—there is still plenty of opportunity for gratification in this process; it just happens in stages rather than instantaneously.

Throughout my own journey of developing positive core beliefs, I learned to celebrate incremental improvements, and that made the process feel less arduous. For instance, when I first started my mental transformation, I would spend a majority of my day obsessing over the fact that I thought I would never be enough for anyone, and I would make mental lists of all the reasons why I believed this to be true. This was all day. Usually, I would have about thirty minutes where I would entertain the idea that maybe I was enough and I did matter; this would then lead me to challenging those negative thoughts that were leading to detrimental core beliefs about myself. Only thirty minutes of the eighteen hours I was awake would I find relief from that self-loathing, but I would celebrate those thirty minutes like nobody's business! To me, that was gratifying!

Although I didn't have a completely transformed mind yet, I was on the path to developing new core beliefs about myself. I wasn't there yet, but I was heading in the right direction. This process was really the first invitation that I accepted to my own personal development. It was through this process that I found myself viewing the journey of life through a different lens for the first time…the lens of hope.

Steps to Take Right Now

So far, we've covered a lot about core beliefs. What they look like, where they come from, but let's talk about some specific steps you can take right now to help you on your journey to changing those negative core beliefs to positive ones. I mentioned earlier in this chapter about the importance of making a list of your negative thoughts throughout the day. Let's make sure you do that first. Now, after that list has been created and you've separated your reality from those irrational thoughts, it's time to take the next step...

Time to break out the good old downward-arrow question-and-answer model. This model is a simple, yet extremely telling process that helps us to identify the core belief that is behind our negative and irrational thinking. Although this method doesn't guarantee we'll find out the core belief that's behind our negative thought process, it will provide clarity and kick-start our self-awareness process. The best thing about this technique is that you can do this anywhere and anytime. In the car, on a lunch break, before you go to bed, anywhere.

Let's dive in! So, let's say you have a situation where you're seeking a relationship, but you have been alone for a while. You might feel bombarded with automatic negative self-talk such as, "I'm broken; no one will ever love me"; "I'm going to be alone for the rest of my life"; "I'm obviously not meant to be with someone." Let's take one of these thoughts and begin to question it and see what this process reveals:

"I'm broken, no one will ever love me."

Why?

"Because I've never had a long-term relationship before; everyone always leaves me."

Why?

"I always seem to assume they will leave me because I don't feel like I'm good enough for them, so I push them away until they leave."

Why?

"Because I don't feel confident in the person I am."

Why?

"Because I've always felt I'm not enough the way I am."

Why?

"Because everyone else seems to get everything but me."

Why?

"Because all I see are great things being posted and talked about by everyone else all the time."

Why?

"Because I spend time with these people and listen to what they say, and I care about what their opinions are of me."

Why?

"Because I want to fit in, and I want everyone to like me."

Why?

"Because I feel like these people have everything together, and I want to be like them; I want to have everything together."

Why?

"Because I feel inferior to everyone else, so why would anyone want to be with me..."

Ding! Ding! Ding! We've got ourselves a core belief uncovered, my friends! You can see how this type of questioning allows us to keep diving deeper into how we feel about ourselves until we strike that ever-so-elusive core belief. In this case it's "I'm inferior to everyone." This was just an example, so if you are trying this in your life and you aren't able to identify a core belief, do not worry! By using this type of questioning and challenging these types of thoughts, you're on the right track to doing so. Perhaps you need the help of a mental health professional, a family member, or even a friend to help you uncover more. Guess what? That's great! There is absolutely nothing wrong with seeking out additional help; actually, it's one of the best things you can do if you feel comfortable doing so. However, not everyone is comfortable with that, and that's why this book provides inspiration and legitimate practices for you to use too.

To continue this process, we want to create what I call *action goals* that we can use to hold ourselves accountable every day. I know this sounds like boring professor or teacher talk, but creating these goals will make a huge difference for us on this journey of changing our core beliefs. These goals don't have to be super specific or advanced, but they must require action on our part every day, an action that is going to move us toward self-awareness of our thoughts and feelings. Personally, I write my action goals on sticky notes that I place on my fridge every night before I go to bed. That way, one of the first thing I see in the morning are these goals.

These goals have to be apropos to what you're dealing with, so if you are battling with feeling inferior to others, an example of one of these goals could be as follows: "Today, every time I start speaking negative thoughts to myself, I will stop and repeat, 'I am enough,'; 'I make an impact on those around me'; 'I'm running my own race against me, not anyone else." Simply repeating three positive affirmations to yourself during a time when negative thoughts are threatening to swallow your mind, is a prime example of an action goal that can be exercised throughout your day.

When you're coming up with these goals, make sure they have these three key components. They are as follows: **positive, self-affirming, and flexible**. Action goals have to be positive because we are trying to combat the self-doubt and negativity that is threatening to take our happiness each day. They must be self-affirming, because we have to work on genuinely believing what we're saying to ourselves. Finally, they have to be flexible. Not every day is going to pan out exactly how we'd prefer, and when a difficult situation comes upon us, our action goals must be able to adapt to the situation. You wouldn't want a goal whose only focus is on combatting your insecurity when the day is serving you up a nice platter of self-doubt, right? Just as you have to learn to adapt to your day, so do your goals.

Core beliefs can be tricky, and changing them can sometimes feel like taking one step forward followed by two steps back. When you're dealing with a belief that you've held for many years about yourself, the world, or the people in it, it's not going to change overnight. You can be as sure as sugar it's not going down without a fight. Yet, core beliefs can be changed. What's important to know is that you have everything you need to change these beliefs within you right now! Don't listen to those loud and obnoxious voices in your head saying you're too far gone or you don't have what it takes. No sir! Those voices are all bark and no bite. Those voices are merely a distraction, don't listen to them! They're trying to keep you from acknowledging the encouraging whispers of your soul, the whispers of "yes you can do this."

Let me reiterate that: You can do this. You will do this. You are doing this. Those are the whispers coming from within; let those whispers move from your soul to your head, and from your head to your feelings, and from your feelings to your actions. One step at a time is how almost everything gets accomplished in this life, and by acknowledging your desire to change those negative core beliefs, you've already taken that first step forward.

CHAPTER TWO

SELF-PERCEPTION SABOTAGE

*I feel like we all have two battles or two enemies going on.
One is with the man across from you, the second is with the
man inside of you. I think once you control the one inside
of you, the one across from you really doesn't matter...*
—Tony Romo

Self-perception is an interesting thing, isn't it? I can't speak for you, but for me, it seems how I view myself changes on a daily basis. My view seems so dependent on circumstances and whether things are going well for me in life or not. It's quite exhausting at times trying to find that inner nirvana and resist the temptation to go to war against who I see staring back at me in the mirror. But this is nothing new for me. I can remember a time when my self-perception was so skewed that I couldn't even recognize compliments from others, because I couldn't see anything good in myself.

During my high school years, I didn't know much about myself. I was like most adolescents trying to find their way; however, I had no trouble identifying all the things I most certainly was *not*. That list included traits such as handsome, desirable, funny, likeable, worthy, successful, meaningful...these were just a few that topped the list of what I *thought* I wasn't. I always believed I was none of these things because of different experiences that I had interpreted as failures. Listing all these experiences could be a book in itself, but I do recall one example that sums up my high school self quite well.

I remember during my junior year, I had a crush on one of the most popular girls in the grade, and by some miracle we had a class together. My mission that semester was to slowly but surely start to make myself known to her and maybe even talk to her if I was feeling really bold. This was the plan, and I was going to execute it to perfection. Nevertheless, weeks went by without me even venturing to the same side of the room as her. Not only that, every time I stepped into the room, my anxiety would be so intense that I would feel like throwing up the entire class period. This constant anxiety was followed up by extreme relief, mixed with intense regret as the period ended without me saying anything to her.

I began to take all my disappointment and turn it inward, telling myself that I was a pathetic nobody and she would never want to talk to me anyways, so what's the point? Weeks went by where I became angry and wouldn't even acknowledge her…even though she never had acknowledged me anyway, but in my mind, I was giving her the cold shoulder. However, as the semester was coming to a close, I decided to go for broke and step out of my daily anxious and self-loathing state in hopes of making a connection. There were only two weeks left in which I would have class with her, so I figured if anything went wrong, who cares? I wouldn't have to see her again.

So, one day, I got to class early and took an open desk next to her. I was ecstatic! I couldn't believe I had finally made such a power move! Wow! I was well on my way to this girl realizing I was the school's best-kept secret, and she was going to be the lucky one to discover me. With that being said, I didn't speak a word to her that day. In fact, I got that same desk the entire week, and I didn't say anything to her, not even asking for an extra pencil, nothing.

As each day moved on, and the semester was coming to an end, I felt my time running out. I was worried I would never get another chance to make myself known to this girl again. I knew something had to give if I was ever going to live with myself. As a result, despite my better judgment, I made up my mind that on Monday (which was the start of the last week of the semester) I was going to talk to her…Spoiler alert, I did talk to her. I somehow worked up the courage on the last day of the semester, and I got her number! I figured I was golden and my time had come. Life at that moment seemed so glorious, I felt like I was on top of the world and had finally defeated my own self-doubt. I felt like I was on cloud nine, and I couldn't wait to see what would happen next! I started envisioning us going out on dates, then becoming a couple, then getting married. It was all coming together, and I couldn't have been happier… That is, until I texted her the next day…

After waiting four days, hoping for a late response, I came to grips with the fact that I had been stone-cold ghosted. It turns out this girl had a boyfriend who was in the grade above me, and they had been dating for over a year. (This was news to me.) I felt completely mortified by my decision to talk to this girl, and it was at that moment that I started to take all that pain, hurt, and jealousy that I felt and turned it inward. My self-perception became distorted beyond any recognition, and I fell victim to constant mental self-punishing of myself for my failed attempt at a high school romance. It was as if the inner man inside me was using this failed attempt as a torture device to antagonize my brain day and night without mercy.

In the months to follow, I started consuming a steady diet of antagonistic, negative self-talk from myself. Thoughts and phrases such as "You're a pathetic loser who will be alone forever, Scott"; "There isn't a single thing you can do right in this world, Scott; you're nothing and always will be"; "Everyone thinks you're a pathetic disgrace; everyone hates you and is laughing whenever they see you." These thoughts were constant and seemed inescapable, no matter what I tried to do, or where I turned. By enjoying a heavy helping of these thoughts for breakfast, lunch, and dinner, I quickly wrecked the perception I had of myself. I went from seeing myself as a hidden gem that hadn't gotten his opportunity yet, to seeing myself as a complete reject who had no value to offer anyone. This mental transformation was engrained into my head daily, and with every failure or rejection of any kind, more evidence was provided to myself that these intrusive, self-debilitating thoughts were indeed all true.

When I think back to these days, I shake my head because of what I know now, but at the same time, I still see myself struggling from time to time with my self-perception. The difference is now I know the source, and I can pinpoint what's causing the onslaught of negative self-talk. Personally, I never thought that I could ever regain control over my brain or thoughts, and I certainly never believed that I would ever shake the insecurity and ruin that followed me every step.

However, as I grew older and experienced more life, I found that my self-perception was still stuck in the past, even though I was years removed from those high school days. Even though I had experienced so much life and clearly was no longer that same high school kid who hated himself, I still viewed myself as if I was. In a way, it's kind of like that old movie *Freaky Friday* with Lindsey Lohan and Jamie Lee Curtis. I would wake up and see a completely different person in the mirror than what I felt like on the inside. To everyone else, I appeared to be a young man who was brimming with confidence and optimism about his life. But on the inside, I saw the same seventeen-year-old kid who had convinced himself he was eternally worthless.

Have you ever felt that way before? Like the world sees you as this one person, yet you see yourself as the complete and polar opposite? Those types of days when people are complimenting you because of something you've done or how you look, yet you can't accept a single kind word because you permanently see yourself at your worst? It's moments like that where even the warm words of those closest to you still fail to penetrate through the icy cold shell of disdain you've trapped yourself in. It's a lonely place to be, and it's a scary place to be. However, just because that place is all you've ever known, doesn't mean you can't break free from it and begin to see what you desire, rather than what you fear.

Being a speaker in the mental health field the past six years has taught me so much and I'm incredible grateful for all I've learned. But without a doubt, the most common piece of knowledge I've picked up from numerous counselors, therapists, and mental health clinicians that I've worked with, is the importance of identifying situations that are going to trigger an anxious or negative response from the brain. This identifying process can be applied to almost any mental health challenge, whether that be PTSD, panic attacks, clinical depression, or something else—the list goes on and on.

That same identification piece I just mentioned also applies to our self-perception and how we feel about who we are on a daily basis. Just as being mindful of triggers when dealing with PTSD is vitally important, that same idea comes into play when dealing with a negative self-perception. Now, when I say words like "mindful" and "triggers," I'm not suggesting sitting around crisscross applesauce and telling everyone on the street to stop being mean and providing them with a three-page list of all our triggers before speaking in our direction. Uh, no. The fact is, we can't always avoid triggers in life, but rather, it's imperative to learn how to identify, assess, and properly cope with them.

This also applies for protecting our self-perception. In the case where fleeing the situation isn't an option, the next steps are to identify the situation, access what's really going on, and properly cope, as I mentioned above. For example, maybe you run into a former boyfriend or girlfriend in the grocery store. Let's say the end of this relationship made you feel worthless and self-conscious about your ability to be a good partner because of hurtful comments made by this ex during the breakup process. As you see this ex approaching, your mind immediately goes back to those old familiar thoughts of inferiority, self-loathing, and worthlessness that you felt after the breakup. It's as if your mind has planted itself back in time, but your body is still stuck in the present moment. It's in this moment where you must fight back. I say fight back because it can often feel like it takes all your energy to keep a positive self-perception in moments like this. However, it can be done! Let's go through the progression.

Step one is to identify what's going on. Let's access the initial thoughts swimming around in your head. Maybe they are the old self-detrimental thoughts from the past, such as "You're nothing"; "You'll never be happy again"; "You're not good enough for this person." Make sure these thoughts are acknowledged and not suppressed, because suppression always leads to regression. Instead of suppressing them, accept that these thoughts are occurring, but make sure not to take the bait of letting them compromise your current self-perception. Remember those thoughts were in the past; this situation is in the present. The situations are not the same, and you're not the same.

Now comes **step two**: time to fight back against your thoughts in the moment. In order to combat this, you need to find a way to pause and bring yourself back to rational thinking. One way to do this could be to stop and act like you're tying your shoe in order to mumble words to yourself such as "I am not the same person I used to be" or "the past is over, and I'm in the present right now." Saying these phrases to yourself brings you back to the present moment and rational thoughts, rather than stewing in those past emotional-based ones.

Now, after the first two steps, comes the final step of the process, **Step three**, which is coping in a healthy way. Understand that coping in the moment and coping afterward are two different processes, but let's focus on coping in the moment. This looks a little different for everyone, depending upon the situation. Perhaps a small conversation occurred and you exchanged pleasantries, or maybe you both ignored each other. Whatever the case, the moments following the interaction are a breeding ground for succumbing to negative self-talk, if not properly assessed. In moments such as these, positive coping skills get to flex their muscles against that past negativity looking for a place to fester.

So, what does a proper response to this situation look like? For starters, you want to engage in something that will help you to stay in the present moment, rather than drag you into the past hurt you experienced. That could look like popping in some earbuds and listening to your favorite song from this year, reminding you of all the positive qualities you possess. Maybe you call your current partner and tell them how much they mean to you, or you start writing a list in your phone's notepad of positive affirmations and accomplishments you've had since that breakup. These are just three suggestions, but it's vitally important to find positive coping skills that work for you. Followed by learning to rely on them in those moments where it feels like your self-perception is at risk of reverting back to its old self.

When you google the definition of *self-perception*, usually what appears is something along the lines of this: "the view a person has about the physical and mental attributes that make up oneself." I personally find definitions like this to be far too shallow for what self-perception truly is. The fact is, someone can view their "mental and physical qualities" as top notch, yet they can still have a distorted self-perception because of the experiences they collected throughout life and the impact they've had on them.

Humans are extremely complex; as I've said during some of my keynote speeches, "Human beings are like onions: you've got to peel back the outer layer to really understand where the stink is coming from." This is so true though. When I think about all the different experiences and aspects that go into a person's life on a day-to-day basis, it's no wonder some of us tend to stink from time to time when it comes to our self-perception. Past trauma, difficult upbringings, toxic relationships, unhealthy exposure to violence, difficult family dynamics, and undiagnosed mental health challenges are just a few of the various chipped pieces of life that together, create the mosaic that is our self-perception. When it comes to the emotional makeup of who we are, there is always more to the story than what we are currently focusing on.

Just like when you zoom in on only one piece of a mosaic, you can't see the artist's entire intention for the structure. Often I compare humans to mosaics because I believe there are so many similarities between the mosaic style of art and ourselves. Speaking of, here's the thing that's interesting about mosaics…one piece doesn't define a mosaic; you cannot tell what the mosaic is by staring at one individual piece or even a few individual pieces. A mosaic is a collection of pieces that are all different shapes and cuts. Each piece is essential to the design, yet it's not till all the pieces are in place and we take a few steps back that we can marvel at what has been created. In the same way, when it comes to the mosaic of our self-perception, we have to apply the same concept. Look at the entirety of who we are, not just a few individual pieces that we wish were different, or that we view as inferior.

When we begin to understand that who we are, is so much more than what we've been through or the individual experiences we've had, that's when our self-perception begins to change. When we take this approach, it may not change our situation, circumstances or make all of our problems disappear, but it will give us a chance to change how we react to the difficult situations, that lead to to negative thoughts about ourselves. With this mindset, and plenty of repetition, we can go from viewing ourselves as "someone who is never going to be enough for anyone," to instead believing that "everything I've experienced in my life has led me to become the person I am today, and that person is enough in this moment!" Both of these phrases are self-perception statements, but one is focused on a single piece of who we think we are, while the other is viewing all the experiences together as a whole. Just like the mosaic example. That's what self-perception is at its most basic level: how we view ourselves. The most encouraging part of this revelation is that we all have the power to change how we view ourselves right here and right now; we just need to make the decision that we're going to do it.

Steps to Take Right Now

Now the next logical question would be how do we go about doing this on a day-to-day basis? We all know that momentary inspiration comes and goes as quick as day turns to night, so how do we work on changing our self-perception over the long haul and not just for one day? This is a question I get on a regular basis when I speak to schools and organizations, and my answer is always the same: the first step is recognition.

I've found that so many of the challenges I've faced in my life were easier to overcome once I began to recognize that there was actually something wrong. This sounds super easy, right? Hey, I'll just realize my self-perception is lacking, and then I'll have a great one by the end of the night, right? Ha ha. Well, not exactly. It's not quite that simple, but this whole process does begin with recognition; however, it doesn't end with just that. The interesting thing about recognition is that so many of us refuse to do this. We are so quick to point out and recognize flaws, problems, misfortunes, mishaps, and issues in other people's lives, yet when it comes to our own, we tend to think we've got it all together, even if we're nowhere close.

This type of thinking also applies to our own insecurities and self-perception. We'll know that we don't feel good about ourselves, but we won't take any steps to do something about it. In a way, it can be comfortable staying stagnant in that poor self-image because perhaps it's all we've known. The idea of trying something new leads to effort without the guarantee of success, and effort without the guarantee of success takes faith, and faith means allowing yourself to be vulnerable, and allowing yourself to be vulnerable means there's a potential for getting let down, and getting let down is uncomfortable. This is the cycle that many of us go through subconsciously when it comes to this subject, and why it can become so difficult just to recognize something needs to change. It's at moments like this, when we feel ourselves slipping into the comfort that the status quo offers us, that we need to recognize what exactly it is we're falling into.

The best way to start the recognition process is to use what I like to call "present moment self-questioning" (PMSQ). This is a process in which we simply learn to ask ourselves questions in the present moment that are going to prevent our brains from going into that autopilot mode of negativity. For example, let's say that you don't get selected for that new promotion at work that you worked so incredibly hard for. After being passed over, you run to the bathroom and stare at yourself, and you start telling yourself all the reasons you're not good enough, listing all the reasons you believe everyone else is so much more talented than you, and pointing out all the flaws you believe you have. Now, before we go any further, let's pause.

It's at this moment that you need to take two simple steps. **Number one**, recognize what you're doing. **Number two**, begin the process of present moment self-questioning. I know, really simple, yet the power within this is undeniable! The process of present moment self-questioning involves asking yourself three questions; three questions that are going to prevent your brain from falling into that comfortable trap of negative self-talk, and snap you back into using your rational brain instead of wallowing in the emotional side.

For some, this process sounds too easy to be true, and for others it seems like way too much work on a consistent basis. However, what's important to understand is that our brain is like any other muscle in the body. In order to strengthen a part of it, we must exercise it, and like any physical exercise, it's not always pure joy, but many times it's quite painful (especially leg day). In this case, we have to begin to exercise our brains' response to negative thoughts. For many of us, negative thoughts dominate our minds so frequently because we fail to confront them and question them; instead, we'll let them invite all their negative friends over to the apartment of our mind and throw a party. Think of present moment self-questioning as the bold neighbor who's sick of all the noise and knocks on the door to confront the party.

Of the three questions that make up PMSQ, the first is as follows: **Are these thoughts practical?** This question is like a splash of cold water to the face in the early morning. It really wakes us up and opens our eyes to what's going on. This question is obvious, but at the same time, we rarely take the time to answer it throughout the day. When we ask ourselves if these thoughts are practical, what we're really doing is holding our brain accountable, putting it on notice that we won't tolerate any more negative thoughts squatting in the house of our mind. When we truly ask ourselves, "Is this thought practical," we're using our responsive rational thinking, instead of submitting to the reactive emotional response that leads us down the road of ruminating on anxious and negative thoughts.

Learning to become responsive to our thoughts, rather than reactive, is one of the most crucial steps in becoming self-aware, and this is a prime example of how to take one small step closer to improved self-awareness. This completes step one of PMSQ training. Congratulations and give yourself a round of applause and a ten-second reading break!

Now that you're back, on to question number two: **Are these thoughts productive?** This question also follows the pattern of "quite obvious, Scott," yet it, too, is often overlooked by most of us. I always think of it like this: we can get so caught up in all these fancy techniques and the newest hacks and tricks of twenty-first-century life that sometimes we completely forget about the basics. When it comes to our negative and anxious thoughts, we also forget about the basics and how to properly move through them. Instead, we opt for negative coping skills or slap a misinformed self-diagnosis on ourselves, which leads to a whole other set of issues.

The action of asking ourselves if a thought is productive in any way really makes things simple. Either the thought is productive or it isn't. Boom. Mic drop. If it is productive, great! Something good surely will come of it. If it isn't, we must ask ourselves what we're going to do to acknowledge and then replace that thought with one that is. This is the basic process that so many of us forget about throughout our daily thought processes, and it's this very process that can impact the way our day, week, or even life unfolds before us. Again, this is simple, yet it's essential and effective for the human mind to do every day.

All righty, congratulations, folks. That's two out of three questions of PMSQ training done. Now on to the last question of PMSQ.

The final question of the trio is **Are these thoughts worth pursuing?** This question takes a little bit more thought, but also accomplishes the same goal as the previous two; it forces us to verbalize an answer that we already know as true deep down inside. That's the thing with negative and anxious thoughts: most times we know they aren't worth pursuing, but it's not until we stop and really ask ourselves in the moment that we can see these thoughts for what they are.

I always struggled with this third question because I would try to convince myself that pursuing garbage thoughts was a productive practice. For instance, I would tell myself that *one bad test grade will result in me never going to college,* or *getting a C+ in algebra means I will never get a job in this world.* I assumed these thoughts were motivating and absolutely worth pursuing. But I couldn't have been more wrong. When we entertain irrational thoughts, it's like feeding a seagull on the beach: at first, it's harmless and seems innocent enough, until that seagull brings forty of its friends back, and all of a sudden, you're overwhelmed and scared. Identifying and separating thoughts worth pursuing from irrational thoughts takes some time to master, but if we can begin to put this question into our daily thought stream, we'll start to see our self-awareness increase by the day.

Throughout this chapter, we've discussed the idea behind present moment self-questioning and explained the process. Three extraordinarily simple questions with one-word answers, yet the simplicity is the beauty of it. **Are these thoughts practical, are these thoughts productive, and are these thoughts worth pursuing?** In a way, it's a slap in the face in that moment, which, many times, is exactly what we need in order to recognize the negative cycle we're entering in that moment. This process doesn't take our problems away; it's not a magical quick fix. However, it does allow us to build self-awareness of our feelings and emotions, which is the key to becoming mentally aware and healthy.

Being mentally healthy and having a positive self-perception go hand in hand; you can't have one without the other in this life. We have to understand that our self-perception begins with what we say to ourselves and our ability to recognize those thoughts as positive or negative. Then, we follow that up by taking action to replace and question those negative thoughts as they enter our minds. This process of developing and building up our self-perception is something that will take work. It will take significant effort; I'm not going to lie and act like it doesn't, because it does. However, if we have the right mindset and take a practical approach, progress can and will be made.

Fixing how we view ourselves will not only help our confidence, but it will also strengthen the foundation of everything else we aspire to do in life. When we view ourselves in a positive light, there's no limit to what can be accomplished in this world. That positive self-perception that we all desire is already within reach for each and every person reading this book. The only thing that's left to do is identify what's going on in our heads and make the decision that it's time to change it!

CHAPTER THREE

THE COMPARISON CHARADE

Do not compare your growth with anyone else's. The only
person you're competing with is who you were yesterday.
—Sarah Jakes Roberts

Comparison is one of those words that makes a person's anxiety spike. Whether we are knowingly comparing or we're subconsciously comparing, the result is inevitably the same. Discontentment. What's interesting about comparison is that pretty much everyone realizes the detrimental effects of being consumed by it, yet we somehow can't resist the temptation to give in when a comparison opportunity presents itself.

This happens so quickly and suddenly that most of the time we don't even notice. We could be having the best day of our lives, happier than we've ever been, filled with gratitude and thankfulness because of our situation. Life could be just peachy! But then, out of nowhere, one little word from a passerby, a picture on a billboard, a commercial on TV, an Instagram post, and all of a sudden…we find ourselves consumed by comparison. Not just any comparison, but the type of comparison that hits so hard, it makes us dodge mirrors or any reflection of ourselves. The type of comparison that swallows us whole. It's in moments like this that, unfortunately, we don't even realize we've been swindled, once again, by the illusion put on by others in an attempt to create a pedestal for themselves.

Over time, comparison can become such a normal part of our routine that we don't even recognize ourselves anymore without it. It's like we can't give ourselves any type of credit for anything we do, because the second we accomplish something, we immediately check to see how it stacks up against what someone else did. When we do this, it robs us of any joy, satisfaction, and pride in ourselves and instead, leaves us stewing in a pool of discontentment, with fuming jealousy toward others.

This is nothing new for humans though. Comparison has been around as long as humanity has, but the introduction of social media platforms and international connectivity has certainly exacerbated the comparison epidemic. The rise of these platforms has led to some amazing advancements in the world, but has also made it so much easier to find someone who's doing something better than you. Comparing yourself with others has always been something to stay wary of, but in today's society it almost feels impossible to do that. Mainly because of the sheer level of content and life events tossed in our faces on a daily basis, via these social media sites.

I'm not a social scientist, nor would I pretend to be one, but there certainly appears to be a connection between the rising levels of anger, low self-esteem, and the increased time spent on social media by the everyday person. Oftentimes, it can seem that we're not living our lives for us but for the viewing pleasure of everyone else. Like many things, there is always an unintended consequence for this type of living. Comparison breeds insecurity, insecurity breeds jealousy, jealousy breeds discontentment, and discontentment breeds anger. This is the type of progression so many of us fall into unknowingly, by giving in to comparison on a daily basis.

For me personally, I can recall numerous days when I fell into the comparison cycle without even realizing I was doing so, but there is one story that sticks out among the rest. When I was a freshman at Temple University, I had the incredible opportunity to become a paid intern with the Philadelphia 76ers' marketing department. This was a dream come true for me as an eighteen-year-old kid who grew up admiring the

NBA. In addition to this being a great opportunity for me, I was also the youngest intern in the 76ers' marketing department history and the first freshman at Temple to receive such a position. Needless to say, I was super excited about getting this opportunity, and I couldn't wait to start making a name for myself in the world of sport management.

As the internship progressed, I learned an incredible amount about the behind-the-scenes sports world, but not everything was so great, especially among my peers. This internship was coveted by numerous upper classmen at Temple who were in line to start their junior internship program, and me being a freshman (as you can imagine) did not sit well with those who were looking for this opportunity to be theirs. These students especially didn't like the fact that I was put in charge of managing the volunteers for game days (who were mostly upperclassmen at Temple). As you can guess, there was quite a bit of animosity toward me from these individuals, and I totally understood that. As a matter of fact, at first it didn't really bother me.

However, as the internship continued, I noticed that some of the volunteers started going above and beyond, trying to prove their worthiness to my superiors, essentially attempting to prove that they deserved the internship more than me. This I did not care for. My competitive fires were lit when I discovered this type of behavior from students who were out to prove I couldn't hack it as a freshman intern. This discovery of mine resulted in the constant comparison of myself to others with every single task I did. Sounds a bit dramatic, I agree, but the thing is, I was comparing myself to a group of people who weren't even recognized by the organization. I had the job, yet I was so consumed with the volunteers I was put in charge of. I completely lost sight of the fact that I had already achieved my goal.

Looking back on it, I see how incredibly silly this was of me to compare myself to others who were jealous of something I had already achieved. I had already won! So why was I consumed with comparing every possible second I was there? I already had the crown jewel that was coveted by so many; I had already proven myself worthy to those in charge. This type of thinking seems so easy now, but at the time, I was so caught up in that crippling cycle of comparison that I couldn't see the reality of the situation.

I remember throughout the internship feeling so uptight and anxious on game days, that I would sweat through the suit I was wearing within five minutes of the gates to the stadium opening. I felt that every single word that I said and every patron I assisted was watching me and would eventually report back to my superiors if I didn't say or do everything correctly. My obsession with feeling the need to be perfect, because of how I perceived everyone else was watching me, became the driving force behind everything I did. I was no longer doing this internship for me, but instead, I was doing it for everyone else, trying to prove to them that I was worthy.

This job went from being something that I was beyond ecstatic to get to, by the time the internship was over, something I couldn't wait to be done with. All because I spent a large majority of the time comparing myself to others, even though they weren't relevant to my job. My experience is a prime example of how comparison not only steals away our joy but can completely alter and change our personalities too. Up until that point, I had never considered myself a person who paid much attention to the path my "competitors" were on, but after that internship, I found myself obsessed with the progress of others and seeing how I measured up. It seemed that my measuring stick with which I determined my own happiness was now tied to the perceptions I believed others had of me. This really didn't change until I made a career move my junior year of college, which ultimately led me to the place I'm in now. It was at that point that I realized the detrimental side of comparison and discovered the power of running my own race in life.

For me, the story I shared above harps on two major points: **number one**, how quickly we can fall into the trap of comparison without even realizing what we're doing; **number two**, how our desire to compare ourselves with someone else stems from a much deeper need to feel validated in some way.

Seeking Validation

Validation is an interesting human need that doesn't get a lot of recognition and attention, or even a spot on Maslow's hierarchy of needs. Yet nevertheless, the need to feel validated is one that's subconsciously coveted by every human, from toddlers to senior citizens. Validation comes in numerous different forms for everyone. For some, that means seeking it in the form of attention from the opposite sex, and for others, it looks like seeking constant positive affirmations from strangers for everything they do. Those are just two of the thousands of types of validations humans seek out, but we don't have all day to go through each one.

In whichever way someone seeks validation, the one constant is the seeking of outside approval for something we're doing, as a way to feel self-secure. Putting it simply such as this makes a lot of sense, and logically it seems that the way to overcome comparison issues would be to seek validation from within, instead of searching for it externally. Yes, that's correct. The question, though, is how do we do that? Easier said than done. When we seek out validation from other people, what we're doing, is putting our entire life in someone else's hands. When we fall victim to this mentality, it's as if our whole existence is centered on whether other people approve of us or not. It's like the people we are seeking validation from become the sun, and every decision we make revolves around them.

Far too many times I have seen this happen to people I know, and honestly, there's nothing more disheartening than seeing this play out. Giving up your individuality and creativity all in an effort to be seen as "enough" in someone else's eyes is the same as giving up on yourself, and instead placing your self-worth in the hands of someone who has just as many insecurities as you, but perhaps hides them better. With this being said, there are some schools of thought that would suggest this a good idea. I often hear advice like this: "Seek validation from those you want to be like, and you'll be improving upon yourself." I hear that and I understand that idea, in theory. However, the problem with that type of thinking is that when we're dependent on someone else to give us that validation, they can just as easily take it away at a moment's notice. This is how we become a puppet to the views and opinions of other people, which eventually results in the loss of ourselves and everything that makes us unique.

This scene has played out over and over again throughout the history of humanity, many times with individuals living their entire lives in pursuit of that ever so coveted validation. If only these souls had only known that the validation they spent a lifetime searching for, was something they already had within from the day they were born. Imagine how different their lives would have been if they had understood that. Imagine how different our lives could be if we stopped going out of our way to seek recognition from others, and instead understood that we are already validated just by being who we are.

What if we used the wild idea of "being enough" as the foundation in which we build our lives on? Living might get a little more exciting all of a sudden, a little more gratifying, and there would be a whole lot less comparison. This isn't some fairy-tale concept I came up with to sell copies of a book; I believe this is the truth! That we're enough exactly the way we are. When we believe this, there is no reason to seek anything else from the opinions of others, because we already possess in ourselves the very thing we've been looking for. The difficult part about this though, is genuinely believing that this statement is true; we have to live and breathe this, otherwise we'll fall into the wide trap set by those who are seeking validation through the belittling of others.

This process can be a lifelong internal battle—that's for sure. It's not something that will come naturally to us in today's world. What I've found helps tip scales in favor of knowing we're already validated is asking ourselves the following question: *What am I attaching my self-worth to?* Seems like a simple self-reflection type question, I agree…but let's unpack this a little more. When we genuinely ask ourselves, *what am I attaching my self-worth to*, it gives birth to introspective questioning.

We're forced to slow down, take a look at our lives, and analyze the decisions we're making in regards to our quest for validation.

Too many times we get so caught up in trying to attach our self-worth and validation to a job, status, movement, or money that we don't even recognize our decisions are based on our desired approval from someone else. We'll get caught up in this, then allow it to steer our lives, rather than pursuing what we truly feel is right for us. The idea behind asking ourselves *what am I attaching my self-worth to* is to bring forth a certain level of accountability and recognition of our life's current direction.

It's important to remember that we are in control of our minds, not some person who has 2.3 million Instagram followers, not some person who the boss at work likes better, not a competitive friend from down the street. No, we have to make sure we're not allowing these outsiders to dictate our decisions and choices. Because at the end of the day, our choices are ours to make, and we are in control of that. I always put it like this: Our mind is like one of those big tourist buses, and we have so many different passengers along for the ride. These passengers have names like Anxiety, Stress, Happiness, Joy, Love, Anger, Jealously, Comparison, etc. Although this bus is completely packed and quite loud, driving it is still our sole responsibility.

The only problem is that sometimes we let certain feelings and emotions (passengers) get the best of us, and we allow them to take the wheel and steer the bus in the direction of their choosing. When this happens, it usually takes us way off course and results in the bus running off the roadway. So next time, when the passenger named *Comparison* decides it wants a shot at driving the bus and proceeds to grab the steering wheel from you, that's when you stop, recognize what's going on, and reassess the direction you're headed by forcing comparison back to its seat.

The best way to look within and force comparison to take a back seat is to ask ourselves the question I mentioned earlier: *What am I attaching my self-worth to?* Let's be clear; asking yourself these types of question is not going to fix your problem with comparison right away. Absolutely not, but it will bring to your attention the choices and decisions you've been making, which will help you to better understand why exactly you've been making them. When we understand the *why*, that's when we can take the first step toward breaking free from comparison to others, and the need to be externally validated.

Comparing Versus Competing

As I was writing this chapter, I realized something quite interesting about the topic of comparison in today's world. I came to the understanding that for so long, many of us have been using the word *compare* as if it's a synonym to *compete*. Upon realizing this, I quickly checked the dictionary to make sure they weren't listed as synonyms, and they most definitely are not. They are two different words with two entirely different meanings. Yet, why is it that whenever we compete for something, we feel the need to simultaneously compare? It's as if somewhere in history (possibly with the dawn of social media) people decided that the only way to compete is by comparing to another person.

But why? Why does *competing* always have to be against another person? The definition of the word doesn't suggest it, so why do we regularly do it? It's especially perplexing to me because engaging in obsessive comparison will always result in a feeling of inferiority and discontentment. Bruh, who in the world desires to feel that? The cold math to comparison is this: there will always be someone who has what we desire, and even if we get what we desire, the cycle continues; it never stops. It's truly an exhausting way to live, and I speak from experience as a recovering comparison-aholic.

As a result of my past comparison obsession, and many frustrating attempts to break free, I discovered a new lens to look at life through that completely changed my life. It's as follows: **learning to compete against the person I was yesterday**. Interesting concept, right? As I bring this idea up, I'm reminded of a former keynote speech of mine titled "Learning to Become Superior to Your Former Self." This speech was centered on the idea of competing against the person we were yesterday, and how to compare our progress in life to that past version of ourselves, rather than our fellow neighbor. The whole idea was to give the audience a new perspective while still satisfying the natural human desire to compete. The goal was to take that competition and channel it toward working on ourselves, rather than losing sight of who we are because of someone else's progress.

The strategy I shared during this keynote that made the biggest impact was a simple activity called "I Was versus I Am." The idea of this activity was to list five limiting beliefs the individual had about themselves at the beginning of the year (this conference took place in December), and then list five things that have happened since that time that could shatter that old limiting belief. After making their lists and analyzing what they wrote, practically everyone had at least one thing crossed out on their "I Was" side and was beaming with pride at the five things on their "I Am" side.

Most of the participants didn't notice all the progress they'd made throughout the year until they wrote it down and saw all that had been accomplished. It was at that moment that I helped inform them of their current superiority to their former selves; they just needed to see it in writing. The proof was on the paper, but sometimes we get so caught up in that external comparison and competition that we forget about all the progress that's been made internally. As simple as it sounds, learning to remind ourselves of that progress is essential to breaking free from that grip comparison has on us. This is how we slowly but surely put the external comparison goggles away, and learn to look at ourselves through the lens of self-validation and internal progress.

Running Your Own Race Radar

While writing this chapter, I've been reflecting on my own life experiences, and I can't help but chuckle at all the past unsuccessful ways I tried to overcome comparison. I seriously tried every trick in the book, but nothing ever seemed to get to the core issue of what was going on. It's like I was trying to learn trigonometry without ever taking algebra or geometry…Yuck. I can't believe I just brought up math; I feel disgusted even thinking about it! Anyway, something was always missing, but I couldn't figure it out.

What I eventually realized though, is that every time I compared myself to someone else, it was in an area where I already felt inferior to begin with. So essentially, I was already feeling insecure about a certain aspect of life, and I would find myself gravitating toward people who were exceling in that area. It's as if I was looking for a reason to feel bad about myself, by obsessing over the areas that were already my biggest insecurities, rather than focusing on the areas I was exceling in. Why did I do this? I have no idea, but I do know it made me feel even worse about myself.

Honestly, I believe most of us have a tendency to fall into this trap. The thing is though, we're comparing our worst against their best, so how is that a fair fight? Think about it: people will usually only share on social media something that's a major accomplishment, right? Or they will tell a story about some exclusive achievement that portrays them as spectacular in some way. When we look at these posts, listen to these stories, or read these biographies, we are taking a look at that person's best edited version of themselves, in an area they excel in more than any other.

Obviously if we don't excel in that same area, we're going to feel inferior and compare, because we're watching a carefully crafted highlight reel. That doesn't mean that we won't get to that level someday, and it doesn't mean we aren't already there. What it means is that someone else took the time and made the effort to display themselves a certain way and we didn't. We need to recognize that doesn't make us any less than or inferior; it simply means we displayed that area in a different way.

But remember this: we all have different areas we excel in, and if we created a highlight reel of our best areas of life, we might make that person we envy feel the same way about us. Needless to say, our comparisons to everything and everyone are subjective, and when something's subjective, we can't take it as gospel in our lives. The key is learning to recognize that very fact, and guiding ourselves to proceed and react with caution, upon viewing other people's lives.

A strategy that I found to help with this is what I call "running our own race radar." This is a simply strategy that anyone can do at any time, and it can be explained as follows: When we feel the urge to compare ourselves to someone, we must recognize this by asking ourselves, *Is comparing myself to this person going to help me run my own race any better?* Then we follow that up with another question: *What can I do in this moment to keep my focus on my own lane?* Two very simple questions, but both serve as reminders to use our rational thinking, as opposed to allowing emotional thinking to consume us. This simple process is how we begin to pull our attention away from someone else's accomplishments and shut the door on comparison in that moment.

However, the process doesn't end here; sometimes we need a little extra something to shut that door of comparison, and that's where we come in with reminder phrases such as these: "I'm happy for them"; "I'm sure that took a lot of effort"; "That may be essential for their own journey, but I don't need that in mine." After we close the door on the comparison, we have to remind ourselves, "I'm staying in my own lane and running my race today," at which point we look for an action we can take to help us get one step closer in achieving our own goals for that day. This little process is simple, but it brings accountability to us in a situation when the mind wants to entertain comparison thoughts. That accountability reminds us of the reality that our situation is different than someone else's, and comparing will only lead to an unnecessary distraction and delay of trying to finish the race we're currently running.

They say comparison is the thief of joy, and my goodness, whoever said that hit the nail right on the head. Dipping our feet in the waters of comparison is so tempting, yet the vicious cycle that ensues can have lifelong effects on our confidence. In a world where comparison is all around us, we must turn inward to seek validation first, and then we can arm ourselves with the proper protection to face the temptation of comparison that lurks on every screen and every feed. No one said fighting the urge to compare would be easy, but the road to self-security begins with recognizing when comparison is creeping in and turning inward to find the antidote. As opposed to seeking security in the empty highlight reels of people who cannot help us finish the race we're running any quicker.

CHAPTER FOUR
EMERGENCY JOYS

We must accept finite disappointment, but never lose infinite hope.
—Dr. Martin Luther King Jr.

In this life, it seems certain things just go well together: peanut butter and jelly, sun and sand, shoes and socks—the list goes on and on. These pairs are commonly listed together because they complement each other well. Each part of the pair brings a different characteristic to the table that the other doesn't possess. Alone, each half of the pair is more than adequate, but when put together, they create a whole new experience far more beneficial than what can be offered when separate.

Speaking of this, I can think of another pair that falls into the category of elite power duos…and that would be hope and joy. Hope by itself is a powerful force; it's something that has the ability to stir up the soul of a person to keep moving forward, even during their darkest hour. On the other hand, joy is often one of the most coveted feelings that any human can dream to acquire throughout their life. By themselves, these two feelings are first class, elite, celebrity-level status, that have entourages follow them with every step. Hope and joy don't need a partner in crime to become more desirable; they're doing just fine on their own. With that being said, as great as they are individually, when paired together, it's a whole new ball game. These two complement each other immaculately, creating a force that would make any celebrity couple jealous beyond belief!

Hope brings an element of resilience and can-do attitude that lifts up everyone it comes into contact with. Joy combines that can-do spirit with the acceptance and realization of the here and now, making ordinary daily occurrences seem extraordinarily beautiful because of its presence. Together, they create in a person the ability to find beauty in the most undesirable circumstances, all the while keeping laser focused on the dreams and desires of the future. Ay yo! That's an impressive power couple right there! It truly seems that these two go hand in hand whenever and wherever the other is present. However, live this life long enough, and we'll certainly find ourselves in a position where one, if not both, are missing from our lives. In times such as that, it can be classified as an internal emergency, a time when we need to send out the Special Forces of our coping skills to help find the missing hope and joy in life. These "Special Forces" of coping skills are what I like to call Emergency Joys.

The genesis of what I call Emergency Joys comes from my own experience of falling to my personal rock bottom in my early college years. The following story will take you to the low points of that experience, as well as the eventual realization of hope. Let this be a trigger warning for anyone who feels they might not be ready to digest this depression-heavy material, because I'm going to share this story authentically as it happened to me, no sugar coating; so proceed at your own discretion.

As my sophomore year at Temple University was about to begin, I was eager to build on an exciting freshman year and look to turn my life into the dream college experience I felt I was on my way to achieving. Sophomore year started out somewhat uneventful; life was good, and that was good enough for me. I was being my typical self, hanging with friends, enjoying college life, and looking to dive deeper into the exciting major of sport management, which I had started the year before. To me, it seemed that this year was going to give me a chance to have even more fun and add more experiences to my life that would last long after my college years turned to real-world doldrums.

The first few weeks of the school year seemed to fall in line with what I had planned, and I was loving it! After a long summer of not seeing my friends, it was a honeymoon-type stage of hanging out, partying, attending events in the city, and playing basketball every day after class. In my mind, this was how college was supposed to be. A balance between working, going to class, and living it up in an environment with like-minded people who were also trying to figure their lives out. Life was good; all was well...

However, as the year continued, I noticed some changes in myself both physically and mentally. Of these changes, the first was the acne that began breaking out in bunches on my face. Acne was not something I was a stranger to. I had dealt with it for years dating back to ninth grade, although, it had always been somewhat mild, with the occasionally flare-up from time to time, but nothing too drastic. This time around though, something was different. It wasn't the usual flare-ups; but rather my face began breaking out in these white, puffy, cystic pimples that proceeded to cover the majority of my face, except for my forehead and chin. This was not what I'd been used to, and I figured it must have been a small phase, or perhaps I accidentally touched my face too much that week and this was the result.

Without thinking twice about it, I continued about my days, believing that soon enough my skin would clear up. After all, everybody always said acne was temporary, and it wasn't a real reason to get upset, so I figured I would just shut my mouth and wait for the pimples to dissipate. This mindset lasted a few weeks, but then I noticed another change...but it wasn't the change I was hoping to see. The acne had now become significantly worse; not only were the pimples painful and blistering, but now my face became tomato red, as if I was constantly blushing throughout the day. At this point, other people started to take notice of what was going on with my face.

Every time I would see a friend or classmate, they looked at me with this puzzled face that was a mixture of pity and laughter, covered up by a precarious hello. Strangers were no better; as I continued to navigate the Temple party scene, I found that being around people who were consuming alcohol and substances allowed them to feel completely free to make all kinds of comments about the mountains protruding from my face, without any fear of retaliation. Of course, when I would respond to them with a sharp reply, somehow I was the bad guy who was "out of line" or "being rude." This was yet another reason why I hated the effects alcohol had on people and why I had refused to drown myself in the self-loathing makeup it provided.

Unfortunately, few others seemed to share that sentiment, and I found myself the subject of every alcoholic college kid's laughter and whispers. It seemed that no matter where I was, who I was with, or what the situation was, I couldn't escape the laughter, scrutiny, and small jabs at my facial condition from others. All I wanted was to be left alone, yet it seemed everyone had to put their two cents in every time our paths crossed. As a response to this, I started avoiding people.

Now, make no mistake, I've always been the type to limit my interactions with others because I prefer to have my alone time, but I was taking it to another level in this case. Weekends went from being forty-eight hours filled with friends and fun, to becoming just two more days of drudgery, laced with excuses as to why I couldn't hang out. When I did make an effort to be social, it took all the strength in me to put on a happy face and pretend to be the life of the party for everyone else's benefit. Days like that were absolutely exhausting, because I made such an effort to prove to everyone that I was this confident, charismatic kid who couldn't be brought down by his acne or anything else in the world, for that matter. But in reality, I hated myself and everything I saw in the mirror from the moment I woke up to the moment I went to sleep.

As a way to win over the crowd, I would often make fun of my acne and make it the center of the conversation as a way to prevent others from bringing it up when I was unprepared. I figured if I made jokes about it first, then it would sting less when someone else made a comment, and if anything, it could show how unfazed and confident I was. Well, let me assure you that this did not help, and if anything, this strategy opened me up to a whole new level of cruelty from others. It seemed that by making fun of myself, it gave others the permission to pile on and let all their true thoughts out. Man, did I see the true colors of a lot of people during those times, wow! I found that when given the chance, people will stop at nothing to bring you down. If it means they'll get a laugh or praise from someone else for putting you down, they'll do it. I came to the realization that my feelings were being sacrificed for their pleasure, and that was the most disheartening part of all.

As these weeks turned into months, I found myself in a darker place by the day. More isolation, less care about outcomes, and unparalleled levels of anger covering up the profound sadness that seemed to darken the entirety of my soul. This was not how sophomore year was supposed to go; this wasn't in my plans. This was supposed to be the year life took off; this was supposed to be the year when my life was a cinematic masterpiece that I would replay in my mind during my retirement years, recalling the good ole days. Perhaps the most disheartening part about the whole situation, was the fact that I'd lost all confidence in myself.

I would spend the entire day putting myself down, essentially beating myself into emotional submission with intrusive, self-detrimental thoughts such as these: *"You'll forever be worthless, Scott, because no one needs you"*; *"This world hates you and doesn't want you"*; *"You're the ugliest person everyone's seen today, so stop ruining everyone's day and go away"*; *"You'll never get out of this feeling; this is all life has for you, so get used to it."* This was all that played on the radio frequency of my mind day and night, 24/7; it seemed that no matter how hard I tried, I couldn't find the good in myself or my situation. All I could ever see was the flaws with myself and the mistakes that I'd made, and I proceeded to ruminate on them constantly.

This type of feeling led to extreme anxiety whenever I was awake, and I had zero clue about how to turn it off. This constant anxiety, paired with the inability to address my nonstop self-torment, led to me feeling exhausted every day, even when I hadn't done anything. I felt as if I'd gone twelve rounds with Balboa in the ring by the time I went to bed, but I hadn't done anything out of the ordinary all day.

What had started as just an emotional experience had now seemed to prompt a physical response from my body. My head felt like it was ten times its actual weight, and just getting up to go class every day left me feeling exhausted and physically run down. All the while my mind kept going, running wild with these self-punishing thoughts, shining a light on all my perceived inadequacies. I remember a simple task such as walking down the street to get food at the dining hall would turn into an all-out slaughter of my self-perception. Usually, the process went a little something like this:

I walk down my stairs, and I tell myself I'm doing it too slow and this is exactly why no one likes me. I proceed to open the door to go outside, and I realize it's colder than expected and I don't have a warm enough jacket, so I tell myself I'm single because of this type of stupidity and why would anyone want to be with someone so incredibly simple-minded. I walk across the street and enter someone's field of vision; they look at me but don't smile. I tell myself, *I knew it; they hate you, Scott, and think you're the ugliest person they've ever seen; they're probably going home to tell everyone about the pathetic loser they saw today.* I get to the dining hall, and a group of friends are laughing among themselves in the distance. I say to myself, *there you go—people are laughing at you as soon as you walk in; everyone can see that your life is a waste.* As I proceed to eat, the whole time I tell myself, *you don't even deserve to eat; let this food nourish someone who actually has a chance at succeeding in life, because it's over for you, my friend."*

This sequence gives you an inside look into what was going on in my mind during the majority of my sophomore year every single day. The sadness would turn into anger, which turned into frustration, followed by another deeper wave of sadness that was debilitating. This was the cycle of my life during this time, and after a while, I simply began to shut down. For anyone who is aware of the basics of mental health and psychology, when the body is in that stress response for a prolonged period of time like mine was, it can't handle it. At some point the body "crashes," and that crash leads to depression.

The best way I can describe this depression would be as follows: Feeling angry enough to scream and sad enough to cry but unable to do either because your mind is moving so fast. So instead, you find yourself living in this constant wave of indifference toward everyone and everything, unable to produce an actual emotion because your body is so mentally exhausted. I found myself stuck in this wave of indifference for a while; I couldn't say for sure how long, but somewhere between nine to ten months.

The worst part about being in that low place for those months was genuinely believing I would never get out of it, that I would be stuck in that darkness permanently, and there was no changing that fate. It truly seemed that my life was set in stone, and I had to make the decision to give up hope and accept the reality that this was all Scott Prendergast was meant to be. I was ready to do just that, until one day, something was a bit different.

I remember it was around late February or early March my sophomore year, and I woke up that morning feeling icy cold. Yes, it was cold outside, but more than the outside temperature, I felt cold on my insides. As I stepped out of bed and felt my feet hit the floor, I knew something was different. I proceeded to walk on the freezing cold floor, but I was not bothered in the slightest. Not because I had socks or shoes on (I didn't, by the way), but because a wave of feeling came over me that completely blocked out any other sensation. As I stood there looking out my dorm window, the feeling that came over me was something I had never felt before, and honestly something I've never felt since. It was a feeling that could be best described as total numbness. I was completely numb toward everything and everyone in the world in that moment, and not a single thought or feeling occupied my mind. Nothing. It was scary.

I wasn't able to feel that in the moment, so in response I remember putting on my shoes, black sweatpants, and a red short-sleeve Temple T-shirt and proceeded to blindly walk down Broad Street. For those of you who aren't from Philly, Broad Street is the busiest street in the city;

it runs from Cheltenham Avenue, in Montgomery County, all the way down to the Navy Yard in deep South Philadelphia. Broad Street is the heartbeat of Philadelphia, simply put. The only problem was that as I was walking down this street, I didn't know where I was going, and I certainly didn't know why, but I continued to walk anyway, completely numb on the inside.

I ended up walking from Temple University (North Philly) all the way to where the stadiums are in South Philly. It took me around two hours to walk this far, but the crazy part about it is this: to this day, I still can't recall what happened during that two-hour walk. The last thing I remember is seeing this huge banner hanging over Broad Street outside my dorm saying "Temple University Welcomes You." Next thing I knew, I was at the intersection of Broad and Oregon Way down in South Philly, with practically no recollection of how I'd gotten there. My pants were all muddy, my shoes were covered in dirt, and I was freezing cold with no jacket.

As I stood on the sidewalk at this intersection trying to comprehend what was going on, the only thing I could make out was a song playing on repeat in my headphones. It was an old song from when I was younger called "Numb" by Linkin Park; I must have put in on before I left, but I had a distinct feeling it was playing during the whole walk. Standing there, confused and cold I didn't know what my next move would be. I can't fully articulate how indifferent I felt towards life at that moment, but as I was standing on the street corner void of any and all feeling, by the grace of the good Lord, I caught a glimpse of a bus stop across the street. There was nothing special about it; there wasn't a massive sign saying "look at me now"; it wasn't painted in shiny gold or covered in flashing lights. No. It was just a typical SEPTA Philadelphia bus stop.

However, something told me to take a closer look. As I did, I noticed there was an advertisement for a local hospital on the side panel; it was about the size of a movie poster. This ad was covered in graffiti, but I could still make out the picture on it, and it was of a mom holding her newborn baby up against her chest, looking like she had been rocking it back and forth as the picture was taken. As I stood there looking at this picture, it instantly started bringing back memories that I had with my own mom growing up. I started having this intense highlight reel of memories of me and my mom from when I was little, and as I stood there, recalling these experiences, out of nowhere something hit me like a ton of bricks with the greatest force I'd ever felt in my life. I wasn't expecting this at all, and this force completely blindsided me as it crashed into my body.

Although here's the thing: it wasn't something physical crashing into me, but rather it was a feeling. It was a familiar feeling, yet unfamiliar at the same time, like I had once known it long ago but had fallen out of touch with it. As I stood there completely blindsided by this feeling, I was able to articulate it to myself. The feeling was that of hope. H-O-P-E, a little four-letter word that is one of the simplest and most identifiable feelings any human could ever have. But in that moment...I had never felt anything more powerful in my entire life. The surge of hope in that moment felt so foreign to me because for the past ten months I had been stuck in a place of hopelessness, and I couldn't even fathom that the opposite might come into my life again. But it did.

As I stood there with this hope pouring into me, still staring at that bus stop advertisement, this newfound hope produced action in me, as it often does in people. I proceeded to take out my phone and call my mom. My mom is a school teacher, and it was the middle of the day at this point; yet, somehow, she answered my call, and we had a conversation. We talked for a good two hours, and I told her everything I had been feeling the past year. I didn't hold back; I let it all out: the bad, the ugly, and the really ugly. It was intense, not going to lie to you, but as I let everything out, I realized something. I realized that for the first time in my life I accepted that it was okay to let someone help me with what I was feeling, instead of trying to cover it up as if it didn't exist. I had spent years convincing myself that I had no right to feel what I was feeling. I tried to bury all the sadness, anger, frustration, disappointment and self-loathing to the deepest parts of me, in hopes that I could live a life where they didn't exist. But this moment on Broad Street, made me realize I didn't have to live that way anymore. I didn't have to live in that place of self-hatred, sadness and isolation because I now had rediscovered something that conquers all…hope. Because of that realization, I deemed that moment on Broad Street in the freezing cold as day one of my recovery journey, the beginning of the rest of my life.

When I look back on that moment, it truly was an emergency. I was in a desperate place, void of all hope and joy with nothing but darkness in sight. But thinking of those memories I had from my younger days, and calling my mom brought back that small little spark of hope and joy. This is the origin of how I came up with the term *Emergency Joys*, and now I hope you're able to see why I call them the Special Forces of coping skills. Because it's in those dark moments where nothing else seems to bring that light into your life, when every other coping skill can't get it done, that we turn to our Emergency Joys to pull us through.

Make no mistake, Emergency Joys do not fix our problems, and they do not get rid of mental health challenges, but they do provide us with that little bit of hope when we feel like we've lost it. When we rediscover hope, that's what leads to seeking out help, and when we seek out help, that's how we learn to heal. Emergency Joys are not the solution, but rather, they are the catalyst that put us on the right path to finding that solution.

Personally, one of my favorite aspects of Emergency Joys is the individuality that it allows one to foster. In order to be classified as an EJ (Emergency Joy), it has to check two boxes. **Number one**, this joy must fall under the category of a positive coping skill. I say this because you wouldn't believe how many people get the lines blurred between an Emergency Joy and a negative coping skill. An EJ has to be something that is positive and healthy for us. It cannot, under any circumstances, be detrimental or harmful-habit-forming in anyway. If it is, that falls under the category of negative coping skill, and that's self-explanatory as to why that would be a problem. That's the first requirement.

The only other box that an EJ has to check is as follows: **it has to be something we're actually interested in**. So simple, right? Yet so many of the best and brightest physiological minds in the business overlook this. People get so caught up in all these fancy techniques and clout associated with their degrees that they forget this simple truth: when someone is interested in something, it's going to be a million times easier to turn to during a crisis. EJs are meant to fit the interests and personality of the individual, not proving some professional student's hypothesis as correct. The interest to the individual is why EJs are so effective.

Think about it: if we're in a really low place, how in the world is an EJ that doesn't interest us whatsoever, or stir up any passion, going to help at all? The short answer…it's not. That's why it's imperative to identify and choose EJs that fall under our interests. For me, after I started implementing this concept into my life, the three EJs I relied on were as follows: **eating my favorite breakfast every time I was having one of those low days, listening to my favorite music on a specific playlist I created, and watching my favorite TV show, *Seinfeld*.** These were the EJs I had ready in my back pocket, so to speak. So when I hit one of those low points, I could turn to these little joys to help spark that hope into my life again, and get me on the right path to working through whatever my situation was.

Now that we've covered the genesis of Emergency Joys and you have a full understanding of what they are, it's time for you to create your own EJ list. Remember to follow the two rules: it must be a positive coping skill, and it must be something you're interested in. Outside of that, allow your Emergency Joys to be as unique as you are, and know that these EJs will not fix your problems, but they will help you to rediscover that hope again, which leads to seeking out help, which leads to healing. That's the power of Emergency Joys, and that power is already within you; EJs just help bring it out.

CHAPTER FIVE

MAKING PEACE WITH YOUR PAST

*A wound that goes unacknowledged and
unwept is a wound that cannot heal.*
—John Eldredge

I once heard a close friend say *the preoccupation with the past will result in the loss of the present and the unfolding of a disastrous future*. As I think about this phrase today, I can't help but nod my head in agreement with the truth of this statement. The past is something that is unchangeable. This is a fact. There may be clout chasing people who make outlandish time-traveling claims, but the fact is, what's done is done, and there's no changing it.

Since this is the reality for every one of us, it's always been interesting to me as to why we spend so much time obsessing and yearning over something that is permanent. As a kid it never made sense to me. I figured, why can't we all just accept the past and be grateful for today and the opportunities it holds? Oh, to be a child again, with such optimism and innocence; those were certainly the days. However, as I aged and gathered more life experiences, I started to understand why letting go of the past is such a challenge. Our past memories hold on to certain pieces of our lives, and many times, those pieces have a tendency to look way more appealing, especially when we encounter some tough-sledding moments in present-day life.

What I realized, is that the past usually has a filter placed over it by us. Just like we can add a filter to change the appearance of an Instagram photo, many of us will take this same concept and apply it to how we view past experiences and memories. Some of us place what I like to call a "Disney filter" on the past. This filter makes every memory seem absolutely incredible and unforgettable, as if everything that happened was this magical experience that can never be topped by anything we ever do again in this life. This filter makes us smile when reminiscing, but it leaves us feeling empty and disappointed with anything that happens in our current day, because it will never live up to the *good ole days* when everything was pristine and perfect. Uhhhhh, okay…let's break this down a little bit more.

The reason the Disney filter has such an allure to it is because of the aspect of control it allows us to have. When we reminisce, we don't have to take the time to capture and recall every single thought or detail that occurred that day. What we do remember are the exceptional moments that caused us to feel something extraordinary. Now, that can be something bad that happened—we'll talk about that in a bit—or it can be something joyous that covers up every other feeling we may have had that day. For example, what may have been a half day of joy when we visited the theme park or saw our first professional sports game, can be misconstrued as an entire summer of bliss where nothing ever went wrong. Or a larger scale example, the newly experienced freedom that a college student felt while away at school for the first month, can translate into reminiscing an entire four years of glory where every single day was like a movie.

This Disney filter doesn't allow room for us to view the hardships, difficulties, days of discontentment, or the idea that anything was ever less than perfect. This filter certainly keeps us longing for those good ole days and plays nothing but joyous bliss on the movie screen of our minds. But you know what I find ironic? When those good ole days were our present moment, we never referred to them as such, but rather we longed for other moments in the past that we perceived as magical. My goodness, talk about a smoke and mirrors act from our brain. Sheesh! Essentially, this Disney filter keeps telling us that the past was better and the present is inferior, no matter how good things might appear to be. Wow, so now that we understand the dynamic of this Disney filter, I think we can see how this type of reminiscing can be toxic to our current headspace.

Anytime when we stay completely focused on a filtered experience and compare it to the day-to-day aspects of present life, we're obviously going to prefer that past experience, because we can control that memory. The fact is, life isn't always a movie every second of every day, but when we tell ourselves that the past was that way, obviously it's going to make us feel like dirt about where we are today. Confidently, I can speak for the majority when I say that no one wants their current life to dwell in misery because of a misconfigured past glory. Clearly not! But, there is something we can do to help combat this type of thinking…

The remedy for this is what I call "full account reminiscing." This is a process I came up with that allows us to enjoy the great moments of our past, without allowing those moments to create a headspace of discontentment toward life in the present moment. The process works as follows. Every time we recall those Disney-filter moments, we should begin by allowing ourselves to enjoy them, of course. Memories are a precious part of life, and we don't want to forget the good times; that would be a recipe for misery. But before we go comparing those great memories from our past to this day today, recall the full account of those memories.

For instance, if we look back and think college was all one big ball of constant fun, let's also remember the days spent crying over the stress that came along with it. Remember the feeling of being alone even on a large campus; remember the difficulty of trying to meet new people. I'm not saying this as a way to ruin our good memories and bring us down. No, I'm not a wet blanket. This process's purpose is to even out the scale of our memories of those good ole days. By recalling some of the not-so-great parts associated with the good times, it reminds us that things weren't always 100 percent perfect back then, and it's okay if they aren't 100 percent perfect today either.

Reminding ourselves of that helps to keep us content with current day life, instead of clinging to a filtered version of the past that fails to recognize anything that wasn't rainbows and pots of gold. Personally, after using my full account reminiscing method, I'll find myself saying, "Hey, Scott, you had some great memories back then for sure, but you also got your backside kicked a little by life too." This puts my current life in perspective and prevents me from falling into that Disney-filter trap by understanding life was more balanced than I thought back then, and it's balanced now too. It might just look different, and guess what? That's okay!

I can recall a time when this type of process was incomprehensible for me and seemed like a distant pipe dream that would never be accomplished. When I was in high school, I had a difficult time in practically every regard. School wasn't my favorite thing, and neither was socializing with anyone other than my small group of friends. To add to this, I struggled mightily with severe anxiety and depression (which I was unaware of at the time). Needless to say, it wasn't the high school experience that is hyped up in Hollywood studios. Glamourizing outdoor lunches, blissful hallway conversations, and fellow-student camaraderie was not something that was commonplace in my own personal experience. Full account reminiscing reminds me that it wasn't all bad though, but I also certainly don't look back on those days with a Disney filter either.

During those years, I remember spending many days and nights wishing I could go back to the days of elementary school, when it seemed as if everyone got along and all was right with the world. In those days, the biggest decision was what game to play at recess or what snack to bring into class for everyone on your birthday. I spent practically every day of my high school career flipping through the Disney-filtered pages of my elementary school memories, absolutely adoring those years as if they were my own personal twenty-four-hour highlight reel. Anytime there was an assignment or some type of opportunity to bring up those past years, I would jump at the chance to do so, while consistently badgering my friends as to whether they felt the same. Honestly, it didn't seem like a problem to me; I looked at this constant reminiscing as if it was helping me through the drudgery and torture of high school, and giving me a way to hide my pain with the bliss of fourth-grade memories.

Thinking this way in high school seemed fine to me, that is, until my last marking period of senior year. That's when something changed. As I was getting ready to attend Temple University and finally leave the forgettable years of high school behind, I realized that I hadn't ever given high school a chance to be anything other than terrible. From the first semester of high school on, after I was cut from the basketball team, I made up my mind that high school was always going to be pure trash, and nothing could convince me otherwise. I spent those four years believing that nothing could ever possibly turn out well for me in this school, and that was the way it was going to be. As a result, I clung to what made me feel like I mattered, and that was the days of learning the alphabet and playing football at recess with my friends.

Hiding in these memories not only prevented me from enjoying the present moment, but it also made me resent where I was at in life even more. Due to the fact that I always looked so fondly on my previous memories, I truly and genuinely believed that the rest of my life would never be as good as those years were, so I figured what was the point? I became angry all the time, because I felt that my best years were already behind me at the ripe age of fifteen…fifteen! My obsession with the Disney-filtered memories of my own life stripped away any possibility of me being able to take some good from the position I was in currently. Instead, I viewed every single day as if it was torture because it wasn't comparing to my idea of what high school should have been, based on the selective memories from childhood.

Running to my carefully filtered past memories was a negative coping mechanism I used to avoid the difficulties of my present situation. The result of this was not joy, but rather a deeper resentment and anger for how my life looked in comparison to those filtered memories of my past. What an extremely toxic way to think, to say the least! However, as I graduated high school and got myself ready to attend college, I vowed to never again stay stuck in my past and wish away the present moment.

No matter how difficult things would get, I promised myself I would stay in the moment and find something good to focus on in the here and now, no matter how bleak it seemed. I wanted to live a life where I could confidently say I had both feet planted in the moment, regardless of what that moment would bring. It was because of that change, that I began my full account reminiscing journey, and it worked beautifully. Doing this didn't take my problems and issues away, but this method did allow me to draw strength from my past, and apply that strength to my present. As opposed to, my past draining the strength away from me in the here and now.

As I recall the different memories of my life, I can't help but wonder how in the world I ever came to make peace with my past when so much anger was tied to it. As a reader of this book, you might be asking yourself the same question in reference to your own situation. The answer to how I went about this isn't a one-word magic reveal, or even a quick summary that can be scribbled on a cheesy blog post. Bruh no. Throughout this chapter I've mentioned the importance of full account reminiscing, and explained how that process will help you accurately recall your past, without the glossy or dark filter skewing your memory. This is no doubt a key ingredient in the "making peace with your past" handbook; however, there is still more to this process, and the *more* that I'm referring to comes in the form of forgiveness.

The Power of Forgiveness

Ay yo! Forgiveness? I know that word makes many of us either tremble with fear or shake with anger, depending upon the interpretation we attach it to. Needless to say, the power of forgiveness is undeniable. It helps us to make peace with the burning fires of anger, and climb out of the deep pits of sorrow that we attach to our past. Before we talk about that though, let's first understand what I mean when I say *forgiveness.*

Many times when this word is uttered, we feel as if it means we're supposed to completely forget everything that happened in our past, and walk forward like all is okay and always has been. We feel that forgiveness means excusing someone's unacceptable behavior and therefore allowing them to take advantage of us. This is an extremely toxic interpretation of forgiveness because that type of suppression and "gotta get you back" mentality will always lead to regression in our lives. With that being said, there is no possible way we can just zap ourselves with forgiveness and expect that we'll never have another intrusive thought about our past ever again.

Forgiveness isn't like the gadget Will Smith used frequently in the Men in Black movie that gave civilians memory loss every time they saw questionable alien-killing activity. Forgiveness is a gradual process that, over time, allows the soul to move forward with the pleasures of the here and now, without holding on to the resentment, anger, and sadness from the events of the past. Forgiveness allows us to acknowledge all that has happened, without making excuses for those who might have inflicted pain on us. But at the same time, forgiveness doesn't wield the past around like a deadly weapon, threatening to bring up previous wrongs done to us as a way to make others feel guilty.

Forgiveness is equal parts recollection and maturity. Dabble too far on either side, and we'll find ourselves consumed with resentment or ignorance, both of which are enemies of peace. Clearly, forgiveness is a more delicate process than many of us previously believed; at times it can feel like we're walking a tightrope without a safety net underneath, just one wrong move away from falling into complete resentment or ignorance. Here's the key, though: forgiveness must be given to those who hurt us, but it also has to be given to ourselves. Yes, ourselves! I know this book is filled with wild revelations that no one has ever said before...but hear me out.

Most of us, when asked about something we regret, can answer that question within two seconds. We're so quick to list all the regrets we have. Give us a second to share, and we'll spill all the shouldas, wouldas, and couldas we can think of, rapid fire. At times, it seems as if we purposely hold on to these regrets, flashing them around to every passersby as if they're some weird badge of honor worth wearing proudly. Why do we do this? Usually in an attempt to garner some type of sympathy or pity from others, if we're being totally honest here. Yet other times, we beat ourselves up mercilessly and allow negative self-talk to completely dictate our lives because of our self-loathing over what we cannot change.

Whichever is the case for you, what's for certain is that self-forgiveness isn't allowed a seat at the table in most of our lives, we simply don't entertain the idea. Learning to forgive ourselves means that we're making the decision to cease the constant self-badgering over a mistake or decision that was made, and instead, view our life through the lens of "it made me who I am today" as opposed to "imagine what I could have been." Notice the difference in those two phrases. One phrase carries the eternal weight of the unchangeable, while the other takes that same weight and uses it as a stepping-stone for the future.

When we forgive ourselves, we loosen the grip regret has on us and the decisions we make, while at the same time, realizing that nothing in this world can change our past. However, we can still change how the story will end. The relief that comes along with the cleansing of a fresh start is what making peace with our past looks like. Acknowledging what happened to us, allowing ourselves to feel the emotions that came along with it, but refusing to let those emotions and memories from the past taint the choices we make in our present moment. That's the power of forgiveness.

As you're reading this chapter today, there's no doubt in my mind that you've taken the stories that have been shared and the strategies that have been given, and thought about what it means to your own life. The beauty of reading is being able to see yourself in the shoes of someone else as they navigate through their own experience. That's part of this book, absolutely. But more than that, I want this book, and this chapter specifically, to help you focus on your current situation. I want you to think about your past right now, and yes, I mean all of it, not just the Disney-filtered parts. I'm talking the good, the bad, and the ugly. When you recall those memories, I want you to think of the people who did you wrong in this life. Yes, we are going there, so put on a seat belt and let's get after it; leave your excuses on the couch because we're about to dive deep.

I want you to think about all the people who did you wrong, the pain it caused you, and how it still makes you cringe to this day. I want you to think about those dark memories that made you cry for nights on end and made you so angry that you couldn't sleep at night. I want you to go there right now. I'll wait…

Okay, now that you're there, I want you to try something. I want you to imagine that person who did you wrong is standing right in front of you—yes, right in front of you. Inevitably, you're going to imagine punching this person in the face five hundred times, so go ahead and envision doing that; get it all out. Once you've gotten those punches out of the way, I want you to close your eyes and take five deep breaths. Then, I want you to open your eyes and stare at that person again, and this time, instead of clobbering them with a right hook, I want you to say the following: "You have no power over me; I forgive you."

Whoa…I bet saying that was probably the hardest thing you've had to do today, but tell me this: Doesn't it feel nice to know that person you've been allowing to live inside your head rent free for so many years is now on their way out? Doesn't it feel nice to know that by forgiving what that person did, you can take back control over your mind? Doesn't it feel nice to know that you're the bigger person and can move forward in your life without consulting that mind squatter who is full of opinions? Some of you might be staring at this writing with your arms crossed saying, "No it doesn't, Scott, and thanks for triggering me." Well, to you I say, you'll thank me later, and try repeating that process I shared above every day until you let that anger go. For the rest of you, your life begins today!

It's time to move forward, with both feet standing in the present moment, with arms wide open, ready to receive whatever this life has for you. Some of it will be joyous, and some of it will be terrible, but regardless, you'll be present in it. With both feet planted in the here and now, there's nothing you can't handle in this world. Setting yourself free from the past will not guarantee a spotless day, but it will guarantee an authentic view of what your life is right now, rather than an obscured view caused by a tainted memory. That right there my friends, is the recipe for allowing forgiveness to flow from the pains that others have caused you.

But wait a minute—there is still one more person who needs to be forgiven in order to complete this process…That person would be you, my friend. Yes, you, yourself, the person who is reading this book right now. Yuppers, it's time to forgive yourself, too, and here's how you're going to do it. First, you're going to sit up. I say this because chances are most of you are reading this in a comfy bed all snuggled up or buried deep in some couch. But this is about getting comfortable with the uncomfortable, so get yourself up. Sit up nice and tall before we do anything else. Yes, this applies to you too, person reading on the plane who doesn't want to draw any extra attention to themselves. Don't think I don't know who you are!

Once you've gotten yourself sitting up straight, I want you to close your eyes and recall some of the different mistakes you've made, the disappointments you've had, the regrets you hold on to. Yes, go to that place, but believe me, from pain will come pleasure. Now, after you've recalled those experiences, I want you to open your eyes, take three deep breaths, and say the following out loud: I forgive myself. As you say this, really let it sink in, truly believe it, and allow all those words to penetrate into the deepest parts of your soul. Remind yourself that everything that happened in the past—all the failures, the disappointments, the regrets, the pain—all made you the person you are today! All of it led you to this exact moment where you stand, and this moment presents you with a choice. Either continue to allow your past to define you and live in the bondage of what was...or forgive the person who you were, with the maturity of who you are today.

This choice isn't an easy one, but my friend, you can do it; you can start fresh anytime. That's the beauty of this life, but in order to do that, you must first cut ties with the old baggage you're holding on to. Once those ties are cut, you're free to experience all that this moment has to offer. So, my friend, the choice is yours. Are you going to choose forgiveness, or are you going to hold on even tighter to what cannot be changed? Don't take too long to decide, because your present moment, and all that it has to offer, awaits. It's time, my friend; it's time to cut the ties and step into the next phase of your life!

CHAPTER SIX

R³: RECOGNITION, REPETITION, RESILIENCE

The Eight Laws of Learning Are Explanation,
Demonstration, Imitation, Repetition, Repetition,
Repetition, Repetition, Repetition.
—John Wooden

Learning something new can be an exciting adventure, filled with wondrous joy for a person who is inspired by the topic. Learning can also be a process that feels equivalent to having one's teeth pulled involuntarily. Same concept, two very different outlooks. Whether we want to admit it or not, we're constantly learning. It doesn't matter if we're paying $80,000 a year and wearing an "I love college" T-shirt or if we're retired, sitting on a sandy beach somewhere, wearing a gold watch. Learning is a regular experience that we all encounter throughout the course of our lives. The same can also be said when it comes to emotional intelligence learning.

However, the important question we have to ask is *how* are we learning and *why*? Many of us fail to take time to answer this question, and instead, we go through the motions of whatever someone else said we should do, until we inevitably stumble across a lack of self-identity and individuality. Instead of falling into this trap, we must begin to recognize what it is we're doing, and why we're doing it. Are we learning something because someone told us that's what we're supposed to do? Perhaps we're learning something for no other reason than to pass a test so we can move one step closer to a degree. Maybe we're learning because we genuinely enjoy the process of feeling well rounded and educated on a certain topic.

Regardless of whatever our answer to that question is, the inevitable follow-up question to why, is how? This is a question that yields thousands of different answers, depending upon the individual, and it's important to understand that each person's learning style is unique to them. Many of us are familiar with the old phrase "If you judge a fish's ability to climb a tree, it will go throughout its life believing it's stupid." Personally, I couldn't agree more with this statement; yet, my college professors still only tested my intelligence using a Scantron test twice a semester…go figure. Anyway, it's important to understand that *how* we learn is just as important as the *why* behind it. Once that *why and how* are recognized, the next two parts are possibly the most unattractive, yet essential in the learning process. Repetition and resilience. Before we dive into the inner workings of the three Rs (Recognition, Repetition, Resilience), let's take a look at a quick story that embodies these three pillars of learning.

Many years ago, before all the glorious joys of a post–COVID-19 society, and long before eternal rage permeated the social media world, there was a ten-year-old boy who embarked on his first season of tackle football. This boy wanted nothing more out of life than to play for the Lenape Valley Indians and don the renowned gold helmet that came with it. From the first time he saw those blue-and-gold jerseys, complete with that infamous golden helmet, he knew what he wanted, and nothing was going to stand in his way. While playing in the backyard with friends, he had visions all spring and summer long of catching touchdown passes and sacking the quarterback time and time again. Everything was going to come to fruition on August 1, the first day of practice as a team; this was going to be the day dreams, turned into reality.

After a painfully long summer of waiting around, August 1 finally arrived, and nothing could have been more glorious for this youngster.

He hit the ground running and thrived during the first few weeks of practice. It was as if all the visions he had that spring came true! He was catching touchdown after touchdown and repeatedly sacking the quarterback during team scrimmages. Things seemed to be going exactly according to plan; nothing could have been better. Football was finally a reality, and practice was like a dream come true for this young kid.

However, as great as things were, there was a feeling developing inside this youngster, a feeling that could be described as somewhere in between excitement, dread, and all-out panic. This feeling came about every time he thought about the first real game of the season against the Horsham Hawks. For whatever reason, the season opener didn't bring the same sense of excitement that the first few weeks of practice brought; in fact, the slightest mention of it brought upon the exact opposite feeling…terror. How could this be? Football was everything to this kid; he lived and breathed it, and practice was the most joyous thing in the world, so why wouldn't a game bring along the same feeling?

As opening night inched closer, this feeling became more intense, but the youngster didn't have the slightest clue on how to handle it. Keeping with the tough-guy football mantra, he didn't want to let anyone know that he wasn't stoked for the first game, so instead he quietly ruminated on this odd feeling day in and day out. As a result, this feeling turned into so much more: it became a nervous obsession. As the one-week mark came and went, the youngster was absolutely terrified of Friday night's opener. He couldn't bear to tell anyone that he was scared, but he wasn't even sure if scared was the right word to describe this feeling. Whatever this was, it felt more long lasting than fear alone; there was something else going on, but he couldn't quite put his finger on it.

This weird feeling followed him wherever he went, but without any way to truly describe it, he covered it up and proceeded to act excited along with everyone else. Finally, after he had endured weeks of nervous anticipation, combined with some strange, unfamiliar feelings, Friday night finally came. This was it, the first game of the season! Expectations were high…well, at least the youngster had set them high for himself. In reality, there wasn't any expectations from anyone else at all, considering it was his first time playing organized football.

As the day wound down and it was time to start getting dressed for the game, that strange feeling came over him again, but this time it was combined with a very familiar feeling of pure dread. How could this be? All his life this boy had wanted nothing more than to play this game; all summer he had excelled in practice, yet now that the lights were on, he couldn't think of anything he wanted to do less than play this game. As the boy arrived at the field and started warming up with his fellow teammates, that strange feeling he'd been having the past few weeks washed over him yet again. It felt as if he was trying to breathe with thirty textbooks on top of his chest, yet each breath brought less relief and more panic.

After about forty-five minutes of this, catching his breath became impossible, and the youngster wasn't able to breathe at all. In an all-out panic, he ran over to his dad by the fence and alerted him that he couldn't breathe. The whole world seemed to be caving in simultaneously; panic had now given way to all-out survival instinct and fear; the youngster truly believed he was dying in that moment. As he proceeded to alert his father, the boy realized this was that same weird feeling that had been stalking him the past few weeks, except now it seemed even more amplified and intense.

As this scene was unfolding, the boy's dad knew exactly what was going on and what had to be done to get the boy back on track. With tears streaming down the boy's face, and hypoventilation in full swing, the boy's father helped him calm down and regain control of his breathing, while the rest of the team headed to the sideline for the opening kickoff. The father implemented a technique for his son to try called *box breathing* as a way to regulate his current hyperventilating state. The simply process is as follows: **breathe in and count to four slowly, hold your breath for four seconds, exhale for four seconds, and then repeat.** After a few solid rounds of box breathing, the boy was coherent and ready for a talking to from his teacher father. He explained to the boy how what he was experiencing was something called *anxiety*, and he had just had a panic attack. It was at this moment that the boy, wiping tears from his face, explained how he had been feeling this thing called *anxiety* for several weeks but was afraid to tell anyone about it. After a compassionate, yet stern pep talk from his dad, the boy felt himself return to a normal state, something he hadn't felt in weeks!

Upon this happening, the youngster was more excited than ever to return to his team and play in his first-ever game. The boy rejoined his teammates on the sideline just as the captains were returning from the coin toss, and he jumped on the field for the opening series and never looked back. After the game was over, the boy received the player of the game award from his coaches, and was bombarded with congratulatory responses from teammates and parents alike for his multi-touchdown performance.

After the game was over and the adrenaline had worn off, the boy and his parents talked about what happened before the game. His parents (two public school teachers) educated him on what exactly was going on and why this strange feeling had happened. At first, everything seemed a bit over his head, kind of like they were speaking a foreign language, but in time, the boy started to grasp everything. For the rest of the season, after he had finally acknowledged and recognized this anxiety, his parents helped him develop multiple different coping skills to help manage the symptoms of anxiety and prevent them from turning into a panic attack before each game.

Terms such as *grounding techniques, controlled breathing exercises,* and *replacing intrusive thoughts* became as much of a pregame ritual as stretching and going over play formations. It should be noted though, this wasn't something that changed after just one week, but instead took repetition for the youngster. This process of identifying and working through his anxiety became something he had to practice not only on game days, but all throughout the week as well. Initially, all these strange practices felt uncomfortable and confusing, but over the course of multiple weeks, the boy began to see the difference in himself as well as his anxiety.

There were times when these strategies didn't work at first, times when the anxiety seemed so overwhelming that nothing could contain it. Times such as these called for an extra dosage of resilience in order to dig deeper into what had been learned by the boy, so he could see results come forth. It wasn't at all easy for the youngster, but thanks to recognition, repetition, and resilience, he learned how to manage his pregame football anxiety in a way that he was comfortable with.

As you can probably piece together, the story shared above is about me. There you go; the cat's out of the bag. It's also worth mentioning that I went on to have double-digit touchdowns that season and double-digit sacks. Ayyy yoooo! Anyway…back to the content here…this story is a brief example of understanding the key ingredients that are needed when it comes to emotional intelligence learning. We can have as many degrees as we want, write as many research articles as our little heart's desire, that's all great. But at the end of the day, the application of recognizing what's going on, repeating a learned strategy to combat the symptoms, and being resilient enough to keep practicing what was learned, is how we make progress. Even when this progression doesn't work immediately, these are the fundamental pieces of any process when we're trying to retrain our brain and its responses.

A Closer Look at the Three Rs

Let's dive a little deeper into each of the three Rs so that we can make this as clear as crystal to understand.

The definition of **recognition** according to *dictionary.com* is as follows: "acknowledgment of something's existence, validity, or legality." This is a rather simple definition, and to be honest, recognizing anything isn't a very difficult process, I think we all understand what it entails. However, the problem lies in our interpretation of an issue that we perceive to be unattractive or detrimental to our image in some type of way.

It's situations such as these, when we fail to exercise our sound judgment in the recognition department.

A prime example of this could be, oh, I don't know…recognizing depression or anxiety in ourselves. Think about it. As humans we like to put on this fancy suit of perfection and excellence, walking around like we are some kind of elite specimen that others should try to emulate. Hiding behind perfectly edited pictures on social media, portraying ourselves as "pioneers" in whatever field we are passionate about, living for comments from others saying how "amazing" we are and how we deserve to be worshiped and admired by all.

Bruh, I think I just threw up writing that, but tell me this isn't true? That's what we all aspire to be and portray. When in reality, we're struggling to even make it out of bed in the morning because our anxiety won't leave us alone, thinking about the things we don't have. So, can we just be real for two seconds here? Let's all recognize right now that we don't have everything together, and we're going to stop acting like we do. If we all did that, sheesh, I wouldn't even have to write this book because we'd all be authentic to ourselves and recognize that's okay. Now, since clearly not everyone is doing that, myself included, let's continue to understand how we can begin to use recognition as a first step toward overcoming the mental obstacles holding us back.

Recognition is always the first step in solving any problem, I don't think it's possible to solve a problem or issue without first recognizing that it is indeed there. When we recognize something in our lives, whether it's mentally or physically, that means we've taken the blinders off. However, for a lot of us, we know there is an issue in some aspect of our lives, but for a variety of reasons, we try to act like it's not there or convince ourselves everything's all good. When we do this, it reminds me of those cheesy horror movie films when the one character looks at the other while walking through the graveyard and says, "We're fine. Don't worry!" Even as there's a trail of blood in front of them.

That's essentially what we're doing when we refuse to acknowledge struggles standing right in front of us. Let's recall the sequence of events in those horror movies. What usually happens to those characters shortly after they give that false reassurance of "we're fine"? Usually, those are the last words they say, as the villain snatches them up shortly after. In a less gruesome, yet similar way, when we refuse to recognize our own struggles, we too, are allowing the villain to snatch us up. But instead of it being some deranged killer, that villain in our lives is often insecurity, anxiety, depression, a toxic relationship, or maybe even a distorted self-image. Regardless of what it is, the beginning step to moving past our own villains begins with recognizing that it's an actual issue.

For the sake of argument, let's say you truly are unable to see that something in your life is an issue. How can you recognize what you can't see? The answer to that question comes in the form of what I like to call "Secret Service mode." This is a process of looking at a current person, situation, or area of your life that could potentially be an issue for you and proceeding to ask yourself two questions. **Question one**: *Is this person, place, relationship, job, or whatever moving me toward something positive or negative for my life?* Followed by the **second question**: *Is allowing myself to be with this person, place, job, or whatever going to help me or hurt me long term?*

Two very simple questions, actually two extraordinarily simple questions, but sometimes different feelings and emotions can cloud our judgment of what's good or bad for us. By going into Secret Service mode, a simple, down-to-earth question can cut through the emotional influence to provide us with the truth of our situation. Recognition is not going to solve our problems and make every issue disappear, as I have said multiple times throughout this book; however, it will always put us on the right path toward finding out what we need in our current situation.

The second part of the three Rs system is good ole **repetition**, easily one of the most frustrating aspects of the emotional intelligence process, and for good reason. Repeating the same thing over and over again may seem fun for a little while, but the allure wears off rather quickly. However, there's a reason people often use the phrase "practice makes perfect"; it's absolutely true, especially when it comes to emotional intelligence. Repetition is how we learn to create habits; without repetition, there would be no habits; without any habits, there would be no patterns of good behavior to strive for. Clearly that would be a problem.

The process of creating new mental habits in the brain is called creating new neural pathways. This is a process in which the brain forms an automatic response to an action we take or emotion we feel. For example, let's say for years, every time we do something wrong, we tell ourselves "we're so stupid," and we proceed to fall into that trap of self-pity. After doing that same process over and over again, our brain starts to form a pathway connecting that response of "we're so stupid" and applying it as an automatic response every time we have a perceived failure. Think of it like an old, worn-down path in the middle of the woods, the kind that people have been traveling on for years. It's easy to see where it begins and much more attractive to walk down than having to clear a new path through the brush.

In the same way, our brain is going to want to take the easier path every time, until we force it to change. With the example I gave above, instead of having our brains fall into the worn-down path of "I'm so stupid" after we fail, we want to create a new neural pathway that gives a positive response to an event or situation we encounter. For instance, we might think, "I'm not stupid; I just need to learn this information in a different way, so what can I do to make that happen?" A simple change like this is the beginning process of creating a new pathway in the woods of our brain, so to speak.

After we have learned this process and become aware of what we're saying to ourselves in response to different situations, here comes the fun part...we must add a healthy dose of repetition. Yes sir, repetition on repetition on repetition! Think about it: How long did it take for that old pathway to be formed? It didn't happen overnight! We're talking years of repeatedly responding to situations and encounters with negative self-talk and self-detrimental thinking, which created that worn-down pathway in the brain. So naturally, creating those new neural pathways is going to take some time to develop as well, and that's where the last part of our three Rs comes in...**resilience.**

The first two parts of the three Rs are somewhat straightforward. Recognition and repetition are two things we all can point out and understand. In steps the infamous third part of the equation...resilience. This is the wild card, the black sheep of the family that has a tendency to go its own way, the one that cannot be tamed or put in line by just anyone. Resilience is something we have to develop over time and on our own; there are no directions on how to become a resilient person; rather, it's developed in a trial-by-fire type fashion. We don't know if we are resilient or not, until we are thrown into a situation that calls for resiliency. We don't know how to acquire resiliency until we find ourselves in a position in which we need it.

Regardless of what some two-bit corporate guru hack might have us believe, resilience cannot be attained with a paid course of only $29.95 and a free consultation. It's something that we develop in response to challenges faced daily, while living this thing called life. The process of becoming resilient requires us to fail and fall down, sometimes from incredible heights, and then to get up again. In its most basic form, becoming resilient simply means refusing to quit. Again, this is something that sounds simple, yet in a day and age where playing the victim and seeking attention is the main objective for many, the resilient person doesn't get the reposts and rounds of applause. The resilient person keeps going in the background, keeps pushing forward, failing, learning, growing, and striving. In contrast, the attention seeker flaunts their so-called struggles as a way to keep the attention on themselves, threatening anyone who deviates attention away from them as being insensitive and coldhearted.

Meanwhile, the resilient person stays in the shadows but gets smarter, wiser, better at their craft, and even develops a sense of gratitude toward their struggles, realizing that their failures and mistakes have helped them in their learning and growing process. This concept is completely foreign to the attention seeker, who views struggle as nothing more than a way to garner attention and pity from others. The resilient person may not get the plastic glamour and glory that serenades the attention seeker, but in time, the resilient person lives a full life. They are unable to be shaken by the difficulties thrown their way because of the time they spent in the shadows getting a degree in resilience. Whereas over time, the attention seeker falls and crumbles when the spotlight isn't on them 24/7.

It's at this moment the attention seeker has a choice to make: start working in the shadows and develop that ironclad resiliency, or proceed to shout and scream in a desperate effort to regain the sympathy of those who have already moved on to the next attention glutton.

The choice is ours. Which one will we be? The Resilient Shadow Worker, or the Attention Glutton? Both have struggles, but how they approach them will determine how their lives play out.

After everything discussed in this chapter, I suppose the question may still remain, how does one become resilient? The short answer to that...live. Live life and go through the different experiences each day has to offer. Some experiences will be incredible; others will be horrific; but with each experience collected, there's something of value to be taken away and used for the good. Every difficult experience faced is an opportunity to flex that resiliency muscle we all have. Resiliency is just like any other muscle; if it's not trained, flexed, and pushed, it will not grow, but rather, it will give way to atrophy.

One doesn't need to go through some once-in-a-lifetime tragedy in order for resiliency to kick in, my goodness no! We can flex our resiliency muscle today, throughout the day, in as many different situations as we want. Maybe you bought a lottery ticket and didn't win—boom! There's an opportunity to flex resiliency. Perhaps you received a test grade back, and you didn't do as well as you liked—boom! There's another opportunity for resiliency. Maybe you spent too much time on TikTok, and now you feel insignificant—bam! There's another opportunity to let resiliency shine.

We do not have to go wandering off in the mountains somewhere to discover this resiliency; it's already within us right now. We just have to make the decision to resist the trap of self-pity and allow ourselves to view every situation as a building block rather than a stumbling block. How does one begin this process? By using a little something called the three Rs. Sound familiar at all? Recognition, repetition, and resilience. The three keys to taking the struggles life gives us and turning them into something beautiful.

CHAPTER SEVEN

THE CIRCUMSTANCE AND ENVIRONMENT TRAP

*You must take personal responsibility. You cannot change
the circumstances, the seasons, or the wind, but you can
change yourself. That is something you have charge of.*
—Jim Rohn

In this world, there are countless factors outside of our control. The weather, the outcome of a game we're watching on TV, the decision of a company to discontinue your favorite breakfast bar (a personal gripe of mine)…the list could go on for hours. Control is something that humans desire more than almost anything else, yet it's something we rarely have on a consistent basis.

What's even scarier than the lack of control we have, is what we become when we find a way to acquire it. Perhaps that's why people pursue control so often, because of the ability to enforce their ideas on others. Unfortunately, we see this play out on a worldwide scale almost every day. The story is as old as time. Power-hungry rulers taking control and exercising it on those who are less fortunate. Needless to say, control is something that is subconsciously sought after by every human on this planet, and every human who will ever live on this planet.

What's interesting, though, is what happens when we divert our attention away from seeking control of every aspect of life and instead focus on acceptance of the areas we cannot control. It's at this moment that we unlock a new level of self-awareness and peace, two things that are absolutely essential to living a fulfilling life. Now, I need everyone to understand that when I say *acceptance*, I don't mean giving up on a certain area and saying, "Oh well, I tried. I guess nothing will ever work out." No, not at all. What I mean is taking the energy and focus that's been breeding frustration in a certain area outside our control, and instead redirecting that effort into something that's within our control.

Think about it: if we spend all our time and energy trying to control the weather, we're going to be wasting our lives stomping around frustrated and annoyed, because no matter how hard we try, that's an area we don't have control over. When we stand around beating our heads against the wall again and again trying to control the uncontrollable, it gets us nowhere. With that being said, the opposite train of thought suggests that being selective with what we try to control will result in a more satisfying and less frustrating life.

So, the next time you find yourself overcome with frustration at the lack of control in a situation, step back and open yourself up to acceptance. This acceptance isn't giving up, nor is it the end of the story, but rather it's reallocating that energy and effort to a more productive area. This dance between acceptance and control really comes to the forefront when discussing circumstances and environment. This is the biggest and most fearsome test when it comes to reaching acceptance for many of us. But without going through this process, the chances of reaching our full potential in life are extremely slim.

As I'm writing about circumstances and environment, it brings to mind a story I heard years ago from a man who inspired me to change the narrative of my own life. The story begins when this man was a fifteen-year-old freshman in high school, absolutely obsessed with the sport of basketball. Basketball had always been this man's escape from the cruelties of life and a way to find connection in an otherwise lonely world. As he grew older and entered high school in the late 1990s, he knew that genetics weren't exactly on his side. Standing at about six feet even and weighing maybe 145 pounds soaking wet, his body wasn't exactly built to be the next Michael Jordan.

However, despite his lack of size and strength, he managed to become the starting point guard all four years of high school and scored over 2,000 points, a school record that still stands today. All the while leading his team to the state playoffs and facing future NBA players such as Richard Hamilton, Kobe Bryant, Matt Carroll, and John Salmons, just to name a few. Despite his eye-popping statistics and accolades, as his senior year ended, this man garnered little interest from major college programs. Although he had undeniable talent for the high school level, because of his lack of size and strength, he didn't receive a single scholarship offer. As a result, he spent the entire spring and summer trying to gain weight and find creative ways to increase his size, although it was inevitably to no avail.

He couldn't change his body no matter how many different programs he tried, and he certainly couldn't change his height. College scouts found his game to be too focused on athleticism, yet at the same time, they said he wasn't athletically superior to the competition. This label certainly didn't prevent him from dominating at the high school level, but without the ability to shoot consistently well, how could he compete against the bigger, stronger, and faster bodies in collegiate athletics?

As senior year came to a close, the man sat down to take a look at his options. Even with all the accolades and his dominance on the court, he had zero scholarship offers. It was at this point that the thought of basketball ending started to creep in. It seemed like all his hard work had been for nothing and life was going to keep rolling on outside of basketball. Inevitably, a decision had to be made, so he enrolled at the local community college, but the plan was never to settle there. He had a vision, he had a goal, but at the end of the day he was still stuck in a place he never thought he'd be. He had done everything in his power to make a name for himself on the court in high school and gain attention from college coaches, but it just didn't seem like it was meant to be.

As he pondered his next move, the man found himself still identifying as a basketball player, but in an environment where his current school didn't have a team. This wasn't something he could change; he had done everything possible to alter his environment yet still found himself stuck. It was at this time that he had another decision to make. He could keep trying to change the college coaches' view of him and continue to wrestle with uncontrollable physical factors, or he could change his attitude about the current situation. Thankfully, he chose the second option.

That next summer, the man completely changed his game; he worked on becoming a sharpshooting point guard who could run the offense exactly to the coaches' preference. He figured since he couldn't change anything about his height, what he could change was his skill from beyond the three-point line as a shooter. Over the next year, he would go to the local park every single day; rain, snow, sleet, heat—it didn't matter! He would stay on that court until he made at least ninety three-pointers out of one hundred every single day. Over the course of that next year, he got up more than 365,000 shots. He shot over one thousand per day, until making a three-pointer became second nature.

Even though he was making these changes, he was still in the same environment, dealing with the same circumstances as before. That hadn't changed. But what did change was his mindset and how he chose to react to those circumstances and environment. He worked on his game tirelessly until it was time to grab hold of an opportunity that life gave him the following September. All that hard work and effort had given him the opportunity to participate in a walk-on tryout at a Division I basketball program.

As he stepped onto the court for this tryout, he already knew there wasn't a single player there more prepared than he. Those same circumstances that seemed to hold him back the previous year, were what forced him to adjust his mindset and attitude (the missing ingredients to his success). As a result, this man went on to make the team and played three years of Division I college basketball at two different schools, advancing to the NCAA Tournament in his last two years. Jay Jameson, from Lansdale, Pennsylvania, had done everything he originally set out to do when he first graduated high school and so much more. Truly his story is one of perseverance, adaptation, and hustle— the kind of story we can all draw inspiration from.

All these traits certainly define Jay to this day. However, when asked about the most powerful lesson he learned during those difficult times following high school, he said the following: "When I learned to let go of what I couldn't control, and instead, put my energy into changing my mindset despite my current circumstances, that's when I saw my environment finally change." Jay fully embodied the idea of acceptance, followed by targeted action in an area that was within his control, and the results were incredible.

Think about your own life and how different it could be if you applied the same concept to yourself every single day. The amount of time wasted on uncontrollable aspects of life and all the anger, resentment, and disappointment that results is truly sad.

Learning to be selective with our focus and hustle is something we can all take away from Jay Jameson's story. It's equally important to acknowledge that although we cannot always change our circumstances and environment, we can change how we choose to react to them. That much is absolutely within our control every single day!

The interesting thing to me about the story I shared above is how the answer to Jay's problem was right in front of him the whole time. The solution wasn't something he had to pay $40,000 for or something that he would find after backpacking through Europe for seven months. No, the answer was within him from the beginning; he just had to change the lens through which he was looking at his life. So much of learning to move past our environment and circumstances comes from the lens that we're looking at life through. When we see ourselves as nothing more than yet another person who deals with a difficult situation or just another person who lives in an unfortunate environment, it truly limits us. We allow these environments and circumstances to label us, and then we fall in line with what those labels tell us we are.

Identification is such a huge part of the human need to feel accepted and wanted, and there's nothing wrong with that. The problem is, we start identifying as these problems and environments, telling ourselves that's who we are. As a result, we accept the very least for ourselves, rather than grasping for the more that's right in front of us. When we say things like "I'll always be a kid from a broken home" or "I'll always be someone who's never gotten over depression" or "My anxiety makes me do this," then we're limiting our lives to the standards held by those labels. These different situations and environmental factors may be part of us, yes, of course, but by no means do they have to define the rest of our lives.

I always think of it like this: Our lives are like a brick house. Each brick that makes up this house (our life) represents a different experience that we've had. Now imagine as we look a little closer at this house, some of the bricks are golden and shiny. These golden bricks represent the good experiences, the memorable moments, and the joyous feelings we've collected throughout our life. In short, the good stuff. With that being said, as we look around to the back of our life's house, we notice not all the bricks are golden...Some are chipped, cracked, and a little dirty. These bricks represent the not-so-great experiences we've had in life. The hurt, the pain, the betrayal, the sadness, the loneliness, and the heartache. The not-so-good stuff.

Both the golden bricks and the chipped bricks are part of the house that makes up our lives, but the issue is sometimes we have a tendency to focus solely on the chipped breaks. We center all our energy on the pain, the negative environment, what didn't go right, what wasn't fair, who said this or that about us. We become so consumed in the negatives that we completely lose sight of the gold bricks in our life's house. But friends, it's time we realized something: every brick in our life's house has a story to tell.

Are there going to be some chipped bricks in our life's house? Absolutely yes, but just because they are there, that doesn't mean we have to spend our whole lives obsessing over them. They are just one part of the house, not the whole structure. What's important to remember is that every single experience we've had (good or bad, gold or chipped brick) works together to make us the individuals we are today, there are no useless experiences (bricks) every last one has its place.

It's time to celebrate the whole structure that is your life rather than punishing yourself over a few chipped bricks in your house that you cannot change. At the end of the day, whether you obsess over the chipped bricks or the golden ones, each one has its place, and each one works to keep your life's house sturdy and together. Take some time today to step back, and recognize the entirety of your life's house, instead of zooming in on one corner where the bricks don't shine as bright.

Responsive over Reactive

One of the most underappreciated traits that we humans possess is the ability to choose. We were created with the ability to choose between a litany of different areas of life, and that's a beautiful thing. However, I find it interesting how we react when we are faced with a situation, circumstance, or environment where we didn't get a choice. When our choice is taken away from us, that's when we have to dig deeper, past the surface level, in order to move forward. One of the most crushing defeats to the human spirit is the lack of ability to choose, and when that choice is taken away, it leaves many of us susceptible to negative thoughts and a broken spirit filled with resentment. It's at moments like this where we're in danger of falling into a mental trap that will constrict us from seeing anything beyond our current circumstance.

Have you ever found yourself in a position like this? It's a scary and uncertain place to be. But hold on; not all hope is lost. It's in these types of moments, when our choice has been ripped from us, that we have to realize there is still a decision to be had. It just looks a little bit different than we might expect. The choice is between becoming reactive or responsive to that challenge we face. This is a choice that we do still have, no matter how bad the circumstances look or how far gone we might feel. What I mean when I say having a choice between being reactive versus responsive is as follows:

When we choose to be reactive to a circumstance, situation, misfortune, or really anything, that means we're basing our actions solely off of the feeling associated with our current situation or environment, without thinking though our progressions like we usually would. In short, being reactive is making a decision completely based on emotion. On the flip side, when we choose to be responsive in a situation, we don't make an immediate decision based on the first dominant emotion we feel. We assess what we feel and proceed to make a rational decision that we believe to be in our best interest, in *response* to the situation.

I think most of us would agree that responding to a situation is ideal, but being reactive is essential at times as well. However, that same reactive instinct that is meant to protect us can also hurt us when we stay reactive to every feeling and situation we encounter. Because the fact is, there are always going to be situations that make us feel angry, sad, frustrated, annoyed; that's just called living life. We can't expect those challenging feelings, caused by our misfortunes, to just disappear all at once. Reassuring, I know, but we can be hopeful knowing our environments and circumstances don't have to define who we are, because we have the choice to respond instead of reacting to them. Sounds pretty great, right? Just be responsive and not reactive—boom, easy.

Well…not exactly. The question is how do we learn to become responsive to negative situations instead of reactive? The first step is recognition. If you're recognizing a theme throughout this book of recognition being the first step to pretty much anything, you're right on track. As simple as it sounds, we overlook this aspect so often, forcing me to repeat it until you're annoyed about it. Anyway, back to the details. I'm sure as the reader you were expecting me to share some elaborate secret that I've discovered on how to overcome these struggles immediately, with the least amount of work as possible…sadly, no.

Instead, we have a first step that is rather unglamorous, yet make no mistake, it's powerful. For the majority of us, when we find ourselves struggling, we don't even notice that we're allowing that particular circumstance to turn us into fully emotionally reactive people. If you're puffing your chest right now saying, *Ha, I'm not like one of those losers; I've got myself together*...calm down, because chances are you fall into the second category. That category would be those of us who deny we're being reactive at all. Sound familiar to anyone? Cluelessness and denial are the two biggest threats, because both prevent us from allowing rational responses to become the guiding light for our situation.

Okay, now that we understand the threat of cluelessness and denial, my hope is that we can see how incredibly vital recognition is as a first step toward living beyond our circumstances and environment. Recognition is sort of like the key that starts the car of this process; nothing moves and nothing starts until we first recognize how we're acting or reacting. Once we've understood the importance of recognizing how we're responding toward situations, it's time to follow that up with action.

The action we want to take after recognizing our reactiveness is another mind-blowing secret...You ready? It's to identify. I know, a wild revelation that you never would have guessed in a million years, right? All joking aside, identifying how we are feeling is the next step in this process. It's absolutely vital for us to identify how we are feeling. Whether it's anger, hopelessness, sadness, insecurity; whatever that feeling is, we need to name it and call it out so it can't continue to cause havoc as a faceless shadow anymore.

When I'm doing coaching with organizations, I'm always surprised at how many individuals don't even know what they're feeling. I hear time and time again from people, "I don't know what it is; I just know this feeling is holding me back." Respectfully, how in the world can we overcome what's holding us back if we don't know what the feeling is? That's like trying to hit a piñata in Australia while standing in your brother's South Philadelphia basement. Yeah, pretty difficult to do. It sounds simple and redundant to just identify your feelings, but I don't think any of us are in a position to act as if we're above this action, myself included.

Think about it like this. Let's say you tell yourself you feel "lost" in life, something very vague that many people can identify with. That feeling of being lost is now going to creep into everything that you do— your career, your family, and your relationships—because you don't know exactly where that vague feeling is coming from. Why? Because you haven't fully identified what's underneath that feeling. That vague feeling of being lost really might be a combination of feeling insecure, vulnerable, and angry, but without identifying those specific feelings, they mesh together to create this bigger and more vague feeling of lost. This in turn is more difficult to acknowledge and identify. If you can learn to identify those individual feelings first, before they mesh together to create a blurry super-feeling, you're going to be able to move past it quicker.

This can be done in a simple way, such as asking yourself, "What are my circumstances and environment making me feel right now in this moment?" Or it could entail making a list on a Post-it note of the different specific feelings. Whatever process works best for you, as long as it points toward identifying the current feelings that are stemming from the present environment or circumstance.

Now, after we've recognized our reactiveness and we've identified what we're feeling, the third step is as follows: change the perspective. Another groundbreaking revelation, I know; please try to contain your astonishment!

This third step is perhaps the most important and therefore the most difficult to accomplish. Changing your perspective can seem almost impossible, especially when your environment projects misery onto you. Trying to flip the perspective when you've been dealing with a difficult circumstance for years isn't at all a joyous process; however, I never said it would be. Needless to say, this has been done and can be done; the examples are all around us.

Look at some of the most prominent figures in our society and history; when you dive deeper into their backgrounds, many of them came from incredibly difficult and hopeless situations. Yet, they all exercised the choice they had control over, which was changing their perspective, even if their environment stayed the same. They may not have liked their current environment, they might have had some of the worst circumstances imaginable, but they didn't allow that to make them stagnant and succumb to reactive behavior because of it. They most likely followed a similar process of recognizing, identifying, and changing their perspectives to then change their lives. The encouraging part about folks like this is that they were no different than you and I; they just learned how to live above their circumstances and become responsive to their situations instead of reactive.

Let's say we desperately want to change our perspective, but we simply don't know how. What do we do then? That's when it becomes a game of what I like to call "hidden gems in the valley." Allow me to explain. We've all heard the old saying "Life's all about peaks and valley." Peaks are the good times in life, and valleys are the struggle times. The concept of *hidden gems in the valley* is all about looking at what you have and where you're currently at, while discovering the good that can be taken from it. Of course, when I say this, I hear a pessimistic critic saying, "There is nothing good or worthwhile about my environment or circumstances, Scott." To that person I simply say, take a second look. That hidden gem, as I call it, may not look like a diamond in its purest form right now, but it's sticking just enough out of the dirt to ignite your spirit with a spark of hope.

Let's look at this analogy in a literal way. A valley, in the geological sense, is a low-lying piece of land between two higher pieces of land. That means there's usually a lot of water runoff in a valley; a lot of moisture collects there, making it a lush place, prime for plants, trees, and flowers to grow. Simply put, growth happens in valleys. To bring this analogy back around, when we find ourselves in a valley, as opposed to on a peak, we have a choice to make. We can sit in that valley, sulking and moping around, spending all our time looking at the peaks in the distance crying at the fact we're not there, or we can use what's around us in our current situation, to discover the powerful lessons that can only be found within the dirt of the valley.

Those hidden gems could represent newfound resilience, a renewed sense of purpose, the discovery of a new passion—you name it. Keep in mind, though, these gems can only be found in the valley where the moisture and runoff is; they can't be found on the high and dry mountain peaks. These gems are what give us the direction and strength we need to climb those peaks we see in the distance. If we don't focus our attention on our current valley, we'll never discover the hidden gems and therefore stay stuck, staring at the peaks in the distance forever.

These steps that I've shared throughout this chapter are not something to write down and practice for the first week of January, only to be forgotten by February. These steps require daily reminders and daily application in order for you to see real change. As important as the processes I've shared today are, there is one key ingredient for any of this to truly work. That ingredient is repetition. Again, a very sexy and groundbreaking idea that no one has ever thought of before…I know, it's simple, but the power behind it cannot be understated.

All of what's been shared in this chapter, and this book for that matter, requires a heavy dosage of resilience. We cannot expect to change our perspectives or change years of patterned thinking overnight. It takes time, it takes some failure, it takes a whole lot of resilience, and yes, you guessed it, repetition. Anything, when it comes to changing our old patterns of thinking, requires repetition, because that's what's necessary to develop new neural pathways in the brain. These neural pathways we're creating will eventually make these ideas easier to grasp, but we have to create the pathways first, and that is a process.

That process, though, shouldn't deter us from putting in the effort and energy to change our mindset and attitude. Our circumstances may not always be fair, our situations might be unbearable, and our environments might be toxic; we cannot always change that, but let's remember the power we do still have: the power to choose between reacting and responding to those daunting struggles. How we choose to react or respond to hardships will determine how we see ourselves, and how we see ourselves will reflect in the actions we take, and the actions we take have the power to change what we see around us.

My hope is that this chapter has opened some eyes, and everyone reading this will realize they don't have to define themselves by what's around them or what's currently happening to them. Instead, they can make a *choice* to *respond* to their current situation, rather than reacting to the negative emotions that swarm around. If you find yourselves struggling right now, let's review the steps one more time on how to live beyond your circumstances.

Number one is to recognize when you're allowing a situation to impact your feelings negatively. **Number two** is to identify what you're feeling so you can name it and tame it. Finally, **step three** is to flip your perspective. Perhaps most importantly, remember to make sure you're looking for those hidden gems in the valley that surround you right now. Practicing these three steps will put you on the right path to moving through your valley struggles, but don't forget to give yourself time, and make room for plenty of repetition. With that being said, I believe it's your time my friend; it's time to live beyond your circumstances and see what's in store for you. It's time to get up, take a stand, and leave the garbage others have projected onto you in the past for good.

CHAPTER EIGHT

WHOSE APPROVAL ARE YOU SEEKING?

A man cannot be comfortable without his own approval.
—Mark Twain

When I reread this old Mark Twain quote, I often marvel at how such simple words can reach the deepest parts of my own insecurities. Nine words, that's all it takes, yet Mark is able to touch me on a deeper level, as if he actually knew me. Clearly, he didn't; the man lived in an entirely different time period than me, but it goes to show how self-worth and approval have been a human struggle for centuries.

Believe it or not, this isn't a problem that originated with the rise of social media and ultra-competitive parents raising kids to be little jealous monsters...no. This is a human problem that I'm sure even Jesus's disciples had to wrestle with. All these years people have been struggling with their own self-worth, yet why hasn't anyone really discovered a solution to the constant doubt and destruction that we put on ourselves day in and day out? Maybe Mr. Twain was trying his best to figure it out as well, or maybe he was saying something that he wished he had every day...his own approval.

Remember when you were in high school, probably freshman or sophomore year, and you sat next to that popular kid or one of the stars on the football team? You observed their every movement in awe as they smoothly talked to everyone throughout the room. It even seemed like even the teacher was under their spell, cracking jokes with this popular kid like it was nothing.

Meanwhile you sit there slumped over, thinking of something to say that might make that cool kid pay the slightest attention to you. Instead, all you could do was compliment them; in a desperate ploy to receive recognition, you grasped for their validation, hoping it would result in being viewed as "acceptable" in their eyes. Instead, the kid looked at you like some scrub who had no right being in the same stratosphere as them. So, you sat there and said nothing and did nothing, as the king of the school ruled with an iron fist over the class. You were a mere peasant that was trying to gain entrance into the royal highness's friend group. It's in that moment you realized that you were never going to be good enough for this kid, so you went through the rest of the day feeling inferior and extremely disappointed that your attempt at talking to his royal highness, didn't result in access to the royal grounds.

Can you relate to feeling this way? Why do we do this? Why do we let ourselves go about life feeling inferior to others? A wise woman named Eleanor Roosevelt once said, "No one can make you feel inferior without your consent." So, why is it that we are constantly giving people consent to make us feel worthless and inferior? It's really an epidemic. You see all kinds of people giving out consent on a daily basis for others to treat them like second-class citizens. Maybe it's your fellow coworkers bending over backward for your boss in hopes of getting a "good job, peasant" reply or a measly picture on the wall that says *peasant of the month*...I mean *employee* of the month. Maybe you see your friend selling their soul and everything but the kitchen sink for a girl or guy that just rolls their eyes at your friend's attempt to talk to them. Perhaps it's the kid at the end of your dorm hall who gets sloppy drunk every night in an effort to gain attention from the cool kids, even if they just mock him or her the whole time.

As a society we think that in order to get what we want or to be successful, we have to constantly meet the approval of those with power.

Time and time again we sell our souls to a few people who possess something we want, and we allow them to have power over us, controlling our every move as if we are puppets on a string. It's quite upsetting. We live in a society that tells us to be our true, authentic selves every day, yet at the same time tells us to fit into a certain mold so we can climb the ladder and get a good, solid job. The hypocrisy is far too real for me to handle. Commercials created by greedy corporations telling viewers to just be their full genuine selves, while simultaneously promoting teeth-whitening strips so you can have a perfect Hollywood smile.

So…wait, we're supposed to be true to who we are, unless who we are isn't viewed as good enough, then we must change? Does that make any sense at all? Maybe I'm just not seeing it correctly, but from where I'm standing, it seems hypocritical and toxic. If you watch enough TV, scroll through enough Instagram photos, or listen to enough news, then you will surely think that you're not up to par and need to start changing yourself so you can gain society's approval. It's truly demoralizing. Sort of seems like we've being forced to chase something that's designed to be unattainable.

But hold on a second; what if instead of subjecting ourselves to constant ridicule and scrutiny from others, we looked at only gaining the approval from the person we see staring back at us in the mirror? What if we went through our lives only trying to please that person? Wouldn't that make our lives a lot simpler and a lot less stressful? Instead of trying to make ourselves fit into a round hole when we are meant to be square, we should focus on looking at ourselves and our square edges, smiling. Smile, because there is not a single person in the entire galaxy that has the same edges. Smile because you deserve to, regardless of what this world says!

Think about all the time that we spend trying to gain approval from others…I'll save you the math, it's a lot. But imagine what we could do with that time and energy if we didn't put it toward trying to change ourselves but rather, put it toward accepting ourselves. We could accomplish so much more in life and, not to mention, have a sense of peace because of our self-assurance. Trying to gain approval from others is a never-ending cycle, because we're constantly going to meet new people, or have a new boss, or a new job. The cycle will never end; we could spend our entire lives changing ourselves for others without ever truly knowing who we are.

When we fall into this trap, our once-unique square-peg edges will have turned round in a desperate effort to fit into that round hole, deemed acceptable by society. Some may say, "Well, Scott, that's just the way of the world; get used to it." Well, let me ask you this: What's going to happen when you're now a round peg trying to fit into the newest trend, a triangular hole? You are right back where you started, trying to change yourself to fit the approval set by others, and so the cycle repeats.

So, next time you are feeling inferior to a classmate, colleague, or coworker, and you find yourself trying to gain his or her approval, think about how beautifully unique your square-peg edges are. Look at the one telling you to change, and feel sorry for them. Because beneath their façade of being too good for you was once a square peg who tried so hard to become round, that they completely lost track of who they were. What kind of life is that? Always changing for everyone else, forever chasing faceless people's approval. Who needs that misery? I would rather get up every morning and smile at my reflection in the mirror, even if society tells me I have no reason to. I'd rather do that than wake up every day trying to find a way to change myself, strictly for the benefits of others.

The older I get, and the more I compare our present times with the past, I see an alarming number of similarities. This is kind of weird, because as a society, we like to think we're so advanced and have nothing in common with the people of the past. But for such an "advanced" group of people, we regularly fall into the same traps that those before us fell into.

One trap that stands out among the rest is the desperate search for approval. Back in the day, that meant breaking your back trying to own more oxen than your neighbor so your town would see you as fit for being considered a nobleman. Or maybe it was wearing a powdered wig and buckled shoes while walking to the woods to relieve yourself as a way to show status to everyone, in hopes of getting a position on the local parliament board. It's no different now; the trends and what has become acceptable have changed, but there are still millions of people living their lives for the approval of the popular kid sitting next to them. Some things never change, even when society likes to shout and scream in your face that they have.

However, the mention of all this poses an even bigger question: Why have we been seeking our self-worth in the validations and approvals of others all these years? Whoa…that's a tough one, right? Answering that might require a little more introspective searching than the typical human would like nowadays. That might require stepping away from the screen, the TV, the friend group to truly see what's going on and what's actually leading us on the inside. With that being said, I want to pose that question to you, the reader: What's the driving force behind your decisions, your actions, your choices? What's the motive behind it all? I think that a majority of us would answer this question one way when others are around, and answer it a completely different way at 3:00 a.m. when we lie awake in bed, fighting off the sorrows and despairs of yesteryear.

They say the quiet screams the truth; perhaps that's why we occupy ourselves 24/7, 365, so we don't have to face the reality that we've been living for the approval of everyone else. I truly believe that deep down, each and every one of us knows if we are being authentic to ourselves or not; some just choose to ignore it because they crave approval from others more than acceptance of oneself. Truly, it's much easier to live a life where we never go against the grain of society or cause a stir, because it means we will always have a cushy landing spot. If anything goes wrong, we just turn to the people in power that we have worked so hard to seek approval from, and they will vouch for us. Simple, easy, done, and makes for a very comfortable life without a lot of problems.

Find the trendy, socially acceptable values of the day and age, and make sure we align ourselves perfectly with that, and we'll be fine. It's as simple as posting a Saturday-night-out picture on Instagram the next Sunday morning with a song lyric caption. Easy stuff! Nice! But when was the last time anything easy actually produced something worthwhile? The problem with seeking all this approval from others is that they can take it away just as quickly as they give it.

Think of the cancel culture we live in; most recently, think of people like Lizzo, who was a huge star, applauded by this society and loved dearly by fans. Only to be canceled for allegations that leaked about her. How about Ellen? Her TV show was a generational hit, everyone loved Ellen, she bought everyone pizza at the Oscars—come on! Only to be canceled as well and have that approval she worked so hard for taken away almost as quickly as it came. The list goes on and on for people this has happened to over the years. That's the problem with living your life for outside approvals; it's like walking on eggshells, and the second you do something that's outside the lines of those who put you on that throne, you're out of the club and kicked to the curb, just like that.

Well, now that we've thoroughly discussed society's lack of self-approval and the desperate ways in which we all seek it in others, let's get down to business and talk about what we can do to combat this epidemic. One of the most important points for us to understand is the fact that approval is something that we *believe* others hold over us, when in fact they don't actually. We believe the celebrity's opinion of us matters more because they are on TV, but the fact is their opinion is just as worthless as the opinion of the person who lives down the street from us. We assume that our boss's approval is the most important thing because they make the decision on if we get fired or not. But that's not true either.

The fact is, in both cases shared, we are the ones who put those people on a pedestal, and we are the ones who give them the consent to dictate how we feel about ourselves. We did it. We do it. We have done it. Why? Perhaps so that they will like us enough to promote us or share their millions with us, or maybe because we feel so lowly about ourselves that we need someone we view as successful to convince us that we are enough. Hmmm, well, let me be as clear as crystal when I say this to you…*We are enough*! Yes, we are! Exactly how we are, where we are, who we are right now in this moment, we are enough!

Nice, so we're enough, cool, but we probably still don't feel like it. No matter how many times I get up in front of a stage and shout that message at the top of my lungs, people will still doubt if they truly are enough. This prompts the two following questions that must be asked: Why don't we feel like we're enough? What's stopping us from feeling like enough? The answer to both of those questions is different for everyone, but to some degree it comes down to a simple, yet powerful word. *Acceptance.*

Acceptance of one's self is a back-and-forth quest for most of us. On one hand, acceptance suggests peace with our current situation and allows us to truly embrace who we are as a unique individual. On the other hand, acceptance sort of feels like waving the white flag and surrendering to the idea that we couldn't quite hack it in life. Regardless of whichever side we lean toward when we think of acceptance, the fact is, each of us needs it in order to feel like enough. Too little acceptance and we'll forever live our lives trying to change everything all the time. But too much acceptance leads to stagnation in our careers, self-improvement, and relationships.

Like anything in life, it's a balance between the two. Identifying the healthy dose of acceptance for us is the gateway that leads to knowing we're enough as we are. Going about finding this healthy dose of acceptance can be the tricky part for many of us. Don't worry though, the beginning step to figuring this out is closer than you might think, and it starts with dating yourself. Ummm, what? I know, sounds a bit weird, but what I mean by this is beginning the process of identifying the different strengths, weaknesses, abilities, mistakes, successes that you've had in your life.

For example, let's say you feel like you're not enough for the people you work with, and you always feel inferior to them. **Step one** is to acknowledge that self-acceptance is the gateway to feeling adequate among others. Then **step two** requires you to start making an account of all the times you've been relied on for major tasks at your place of work. Recalling the times you've received positive feedback from those you have assisted, the times you have spearheaded projects that showcased your ability to communicate. The list can go on and on. Please let it go on and on! You need to recall all these experiences, strengths, weaknesses, failures, and triumphs so that you can prove to yourself that although you are imperfect, you make an undeniable impact and are a valuable piece of the team who makes a difference.

This example shows the power of reflection, my friends. Too often we get caught up in planning solely for the future and trying to dismiss the past as irrelevant, but this mentality causes us pain in the present moment. Without reflecting on the noteworthy moments of our lives in the past, we will forever be at the mercy of whatever new negative feelings come our way in the present. The past (as we talked about earlier in the book) can be a stumbling block for us, or it can act as an anchor, so to speak. Memories to recall and triumphs to be recounted, providing evidence to ourselves when those self-doubting voices of the present start eating away at us.

So, just as you make time to eat every day and socialize, why not find time to reflect on the triumphs of your life each and every day? It doesn't have to be some whole elaborate process complete with a new desk and computer, and it certainly doesn't require you to tell the whole world about it on social media…but instead, take ten minutes every day to recall your success, your triumphs, and the times you've been resilient. There's power in reflecting on the right things.

This type of practice builds confidence, and let's be honest, we all could use an extra boost of that nowadays. The point of this little reflection exercise is to help us understand that we need to be seeking our own approval first and foremost, and let our actions be a direct result of the belief in ourselves. When we start applying the proper amount of self-acceptance and mix in a hefty dosage of reflection, we're going to start breaking down that desire for external validation and allow that self-approval to start creeping in more and more. I need everyone to understand, though, that this will take time. As I write this book, I am still wrestling with this process myself; however, I have made enormous strides over the past few years, adopting and putting into practice these skills I've shared with you in this chapter. Take it from me, you will see a difference! Just be patience, resilient, and give yourself grace throughout the process. Above all else, know that you are enough right now in this moment, exactly as you are. You are enough. You don't have to prove it to anyone, you don't have to convince anyone, and you don't have to listen to anyone who tells you otherwise.

CHAPTER NINE
THE DAILY BATTLE

I wonder how many times people give up just before a
breakthrough—when they are on the very brink of success.
—Joyce Meyer

Joyce Meyer wrote a book back in 1995 titled *The Battlefield of the Mind*, in which she talks about the daily struggle that we all face against ourselves. Personally, this is one of my favorite books I've ever had the opportunity to read, and I often look back on the chapters that made the biggest impact on me, especially when I'm struggling with my own internal battle. I think for me, the title just about sums up the daily conundrum that we humans face: the fact that our mind truly feels like a battlefield more often than not.

Every day when we wake up, our minds begin to swarm with thoughts about all the what-ifs, the self-doubts, the "I cants," the "I'm nots," the "I will nevers." It's brutal! This happens almost immediately for most of us, and if not immediately, then certainly within the first fifteen minutes of waking up. That alarm goes off and then boom! We're under siege trying to take cover from the full-scale assault launched on us by our own minds. Good times, right? Nothing better than trying to brush your teeth peacefully, yet all that can occupy your mind are the worries and insecurities from yesterday overstaying their welcome.

In response to this, typically we react in one of a few ways. **Option one**, we try to just ignore the thoughts and feelings that are dominating us and instead focus on the work or tasks we have to accomplish. We hope that staying busy will simply make the loudness of our minds quiet down. **Option two**, we distract ourselves with the problems and Concerns of other people or world events, in an effort to numb our own struggles and divert our attention from the true pain we're experiencing. Or **option three**, we completely give in and allow the battle of our minds to become an all-out annihilation of our confidence, joy, and resilience. This results in a profound feeling of hopelessness that sticks to us like glue throughout the day. These, of course, aren't the only options we have, but many times these are the three that we turn to as a way to seek refuge from our own minds.

It's a shame because all three of the options I listed above ultimately lead to the same outcome: losing the battle against our minds and allowing what we feel to dictate the outcome of our entire day. I can say with absolute certainty that I fell victim to all three of these negative coping options for years. I truly thought there was no relief from the seemingly endless onslaught of vicious attacks against myself from the inside. I remember every morning when I would wake up in high school and college, I'd be happy for about five minutes, and then slowly but surely, I would see my mood change because of the thoughts I was entertaining throughout the day. By the time the day was over, I was so relieved to sleep so the torture would end, and I could be at peace with myself for a few hours.

I realized that the mind, as beautiful of a place as it can be, can be equally dark and dangerous when the wrong thoughts, memories, and emotions are ruminated on day after day. I remember during these dark days of my life I would be walking through the streets of Philadelphia feeling so envious of anyone who would be smiling or laughing, or anyone who didn't look miserable. I couldn't understand why they all seemed to be so happy and free, yet I felt chained to these unwanted thoughts about myself. Furthermore, I didn't understand why I couldn't get these thoughts under control; it seemed like nothing would help, no matter how hard I tried.

I was angry at people I didn't even know for appearing to be happy, because I wanted what I thought they had. I wanted to smile, I wanted to laugh, I wanted to have a thought come into my mind that wasn't self-detrimental for once. I wanted it so badly that I couldn't even bear to make eye contact with anyone anymore. I would walk around the city looking upward at the buildings or downward to the sidewalk so that I wouldn't have to see the faces of anyone and be further disappointed in my own life. This went on for years. I would occasionally have stretches where I would feel okay and not in the dungeon of my own mind, but these moments were usually short lived and very circumstantially based. It felt like anytime I thought I was close to finding some joy, this dark hand from the abyss would pull me back down to the dungeon of my mind, reminding me of all the reasons why I would never be happy.

During those days, my mind was so tainted that I could have something good happen to me and within about two minutes, I would have myself convinced that it was bad, I didn't deserve it, I was worthless, and there must have been some mistake as to why it happened. Living that way was exhausting in every way imaginable: physically, mentally, emotionally, spiritually...everything. It was darkness as far as the eye could see, and I walked around telling myself this story of defeat, despair, and disgust because that's what the bombs of my mind had deployed on me every single morning. I just couldn't get myself to fight back anymore.

As time carried on and I fell deeper into the ironclad grip of my mind's dungeon, I found myself starting to accept that I would always have to deal with this and I would never be happy. I assumed this darkness was just going to be my lot in life. I truly believed it was time to accept that and submit to the notion that hope wasn't going to be for me. It was a dark and cold place. That type of cold, though, doesn't come from winter chills, but from the loss of hope in the human spirit. But just as this mindset was ready to sink in permanently, there was a change, there was an intervention, there was a shift.

I remember I was watching TV in my dorm room, and I couldn't find anything on, so out of pure boredom I kept flipping through the channels, curious to see what the highest channel number was. As I did this, I came across a channel that was dedicated to Christian broadcasting. Now, I had grown up a Christian, and I knew God was real, but I felt angry, abandoned, and betrayed by him for years. In short, my faith wasn't exactly the strongest, and I certainly wasn't open to any preachers telling me everything I was doing wrong, just to get me to feel bad. Safe to say, I wasn't exactly looking to watch this channel.

However, the man that was preaching on the screen said something that stuck with me and garnered my attention to keep watching. He said, "Put on the full armor of God." He was referencing the scripture from Ephesians 6:11, which reads, "Put on the full armor of God, so that you can take your stand against the devil's schemes" (Ephesians 6:11, NIV). When I heard this, something clicked inside me. I didn't exactly understand what the man was saying, but I felt connected to the message and continued to watch it all the way through. After the preacher was done, I looked up the scripture and found the full meaning and interpretation.

What I got from it was essentially this: Hey, look bro, you've got to arm and protect yourself because you've got a battle going on here mentally, whether you want to admit it or not, so suit up, 'cause otherwise you're toast, son.

I realized I hadn't been putting on any armor at all against the war going on in my mind. Not only that, but the enemy of my mind was coming at me hard every day with fresh bombs to destroy me, and I was just letting it happen without fighting back. After I heard this message, I made a plan to put on my armor and start to turn this slaughter of my mind into an actual competitive battle. I remember feeling fresh hope, feeling empowered, feeling resilient, and almost looking forward to the next negative thought that came my way, so I could flash my new shiny armor, and show I wasn't going to be beaten into submission anymore by my own mind.

That message I saw on a little TV screen in my dorm room really changed a lot for me. It sparked something inside me. That message by Pastor T. D. Jakes made me realize that God was here to help me, but also that I could do something about this darkness that came after me every day. For me, the armor I began to put on, was the promises of scripture and teachings of the Bible, but also gaining an understanding of where these thoughts were coming from. This was truly the beginning of my journey to self-awareness.

For years, I had always assumed I couldn't do anything about these crazy thoughts that came into my head, but I realized that although I can't always control my thoughts, I can control how I react to them. I realized that I have the power to either starve or feed every thought that comes into my mind throughout the day. Let me explain what I mean by that. Starving a thought consisted of not giving any extra attention to it, not going down the rabbit hole of what-ifs, not entertaining the accusations of the thought, and not allowing the thought to dictate my feelings toward the day. This was how I began to weaken those self-detrimental thoughts and break free from their grip, so I could create room for the good thoughts to become stronger.

The process of building up the positive thoughts involved "feeding" the encouraging thoughts. This would mean reflecting on the good thoughts, taking action that supported the positive thoughts, providing evidence to myself on behalf of the good thoughts, and adding emotional connections to the productive thoughts I had. This process between starving and feeding thoughts was, and is, the battle of the mind. This is how we fight back and take control over our mind. This is how we win the war against ourselves, instead of being annihilated day after day by the bombardments of negativity and sadness. We've got to become aware first; then, after we've become aware, we have to start the process of starving and feeding the correct thoughts and feelings. These are the decisions that are going to determine how we feel about ourselves and how we view the very lives we live.

This process and the decisions that cone along with it are no different than the thousands of other decisions we make throughout the day. The only difference is that whichever thoughts we starve and whichever thoughts we feed, will set the foundation for every other choice we make throughout the day. That's pretty important, I think we can all agree. That's why we need to work on becoming aware of what we say and how we say it to ourselves on a daily basis.

Now I want you to take everything that's been shared in this chapter and apply it to your own life right now. All of this means nothing if you don't find a way to make this information fit into the uniqueness of your own situation. Maybe you don't want to call it starving and feeding thoughts; maybe you'll call it something different. It doesn't matter; what's important is that you take the concepts I've shared with you and make it your own. That's how all this mumbo jumbo begins to stick, by adding emotion and a personal touch to it, and only you can do that. This process is simple, and chances are you've already adopted it in some type of way.

I remember adding my own personal touch to an otherwise boring process is how I learned my times tables in elementary school. I loved sports, so for every number I would think of a different athlete who wore that jersey number. It was so much easier to remember Brett Favre multiplied by Brett Favre equals Jake Plumber, than it was to remember four times four equals sixteen. For you, find out how to mold these concepts into your own life in a way that you'll view it as a joy, rather than a chore.

Now, I do want to be clear with you all. This isn't going to be a process that happens overnight; I don't want to get a bunch of emails saying, "Scott, I've been trying the concepts you've shared in your book for three days and nothing's changed yet." As I've reiterated multiple times throughout this book, the key ingredients to everything I've talked about include time and repetition. Please don't skimp on these two; you need them, and while you're at it, you'll be developing another key life trait…patience.

So, are there going to be some growing pains? Absolutely. Are there going to be days where you feel like you're going backward? Definitely. Will there be times where you want to throw your hands up and rage quit? One hundred percent. But you know what else there will be throughout this process? Progress. Despite all the discomfort and setbacks, you will be making progress in your life. You will be taking back control over your mind and learning how to fight back against the darkness that lurks around every corner, looking to infiltrate your peace. You will be doing it! It may be dirty work, it may be uncomfortable work, but it will be work that transforms your life from the inside out! With that in mind, be kind to yourself and consistently remind that brain of yours of the progress you're making.

As I'm sharing these concepts with you, I'm reminded of an old article that I wrote back in college when I was just trying to understand all this stuff myself. The article was titled "Experiencing Failure? It Means You're Succeeding." I hope this quick article can help you understand how progress doesn't always look like what you expect, but if we change the way we view our failures, it will help us to change what progress means to us.

We have been looking at failure all wrong.

College is a time of many great joys and new experiences, but it's also a time to experience failure. Failed that test, failed to remember what you did last night, failed to make the team, failed to gain the attention of the one you seek. The list can go on for hours.

Every time we encounter one of these failures, which is quite often, we shut down and decide we never will try that again. We hate the feeling of failure so much that we let it take complete control over our lives, dictating everything from our participation in class, to making new friends, or even trying to pursue a relationship.

Failure really has each of us wrapped around its finger; whatever it tells us to do...or not to do...we comply. We have been raised by a society that illustrates two types of people: those who are successful and those who are not. We have this idea in our minds that there is nothing in between; either you are a person who has everything or you are a complete failure in life.

Because of this we tend to look down on those who aren't at the level we are and put ourselves down for not being as successful as someone else. All these feelings are controlled by the masterful hand of failure; it takes complete control, leaving us in utter disarray at times.

What if, instead of beating ourselves up over failing, we looked at it as a success? Most people would take one look at that line and laugh; your typical business person who sees themselves as successful would scoff at the mere thought of being excited over failure.

But think about it; when something doesn't work out, you're one step closer to figuring it out. Every time you fail, it's another experience for you to put in your back pocket, a little mental reminder that, hey, that didn't work; now I know to try something different for the next time. To me that's a success; you're closer now to finding a way to figuring something out than you were before you "failed." So, shouldn't that be viewed as a success?

We have this idea in our minds that everyone must follow this certain path to achieve our goals in life, whatever they might be. We listen to people who have "made it," and we think our path has to be exactly the same. We hear about all the success of others, and then we look at our life and see a slew of failures. This prompts us to put ourselves down, and that leads to a dark place that can be awfully hard to get out of.

As hard as it can be, we must resist the urge to put ourselves down when a situation does not turn out the way that we had hoped, and instead focus on what took place as a learning experience that is getting us closer to success.

When you start to take that approach to life, you are never going to get down on yourself or become somber over your lack of current success, because you realize that by failing you are succeeding in getting closer to what you desire.

In life we are always going to have challenges that cause us to stumble, and sometimes we may fall flat on our faces. But never has there been a time in history when something good was accomplished by lying there with your face in the mud. Life is about what you decide to do in that moment when all you can taste and see is dirt.

The decision that we have to make is to get up and go after it again or lie there, wallowing in self-pity, hoping that somehow we will achieve our goal while seeing nothing but dirt. The choice is ours, and failures are just short-term successes that we don't see because we are blinded by the allure of a long-term goal.

However, in order to achieve that long-term goal, it is imperative to accumulate multiple short-term successes...but if you are viewing these successes as failures, then reaching your goal will forever seem out of reach.

This article pretty much sums it up; now it's up to you to apply what was said. Take a look at your life and examine the failures; you might be surprised at how they lead to your successes. Yes, this will be a daily battle, but it's a battle you're more than equipped to handle and win.

CHAPTER TEN
YOU'RE READY

*Learning that it can be more terrible to live than to die, he is
driven onward through the burning crucible of desert, where holy
men and prophets are cleansed and purged for God's great purpose,
until at last, at the end of human strength, beaten into the dust
from which he came, the metal is ready for the Maker's hand.*
—Cecil B. DeMille as Narrator in *The Ten Commandments*

This book isn't going to be easy to categorize; I feel sorry for any librarians trying to find a sensible section for its display. This book is equal parts my own therapy sessions written on paper, a guided collection of suggestion for those struggling, and a testimony to the power of the human spirit and grace of God, all in one. But above all, I hope this book is proof to at least one individual that the darkness which seems to stalk them around every corner is temporary, and there is hope to be had. We've covered it all in this book, but now it's time for you, the reader, to take what's been shared and start applying it to your own life.

All the strategies I've covered—from learning to starve negative thoughts and feed the correct thoughts, discovering your Emergency Joys, to using Secret Service mode and present moment self-questioning—can be molded to fit your own unique situation. That's the exact reason why I wrote this book: to give people tangible strategies and lived-in wisdom that's ready to be personalized to them. I wanted this book to be for the everyday person who is struggling to get past the hurdles life has thrown them. I want people who have no mental health education, no understanding of therapy practices, zero clue of positive psychology, and no status to their names to be able to read the contents of this book and say, "Wow, I can do this. I can change how I view my life; I can rediscover resilience again." That's who I wrote this book for. The everyday people that make up 99 percent of the population in this world.

I understand this book won't be everyone's cup of tea; it's probably not for the person who has fifteen different degrees and likes to hear themselves talk to bored college students just looking to pass a class. Nah, they'll probably try to pontificate about some theory from 1874 that no one cares about. Please…who needs that?

This book is for the rest of us, the ones who desperately want to squeeze the slightest bit of enjoyment out of this life before our time here is done. The people who know in the deepest parts of their souls that there is more to life than the current mental suffering and aguish they face today. This is for you, my friends. I hope you take every word in this book and make it your own, then pass on what you learned to the next person who's at their own rock bottom. The journey from rock bottom to rock solid isn't an easy one. As a matter of fact, it might be the most difficult journey you'll ever embark on in your life. However, when you start this process and learn how to navigate your life through the lens of hope, there's not a single struggle that will keep you permanently locked in the darkness of your mind ever again.

So, I guess that's all I have for you friends. Thanks for going on this journey with me, and I hope this book sparked even just a little glimmer of hope inside you. Now it's up to you to decide where that hope will take you, but before we end this book, let me leave you with one final piece of advice: It's your time; you're ready for all that life has to offer, and it's time to grasp it with both hands. The day is yours, so seize it for what it is! Seize it for the good, the bad, the ugly, and the beautiful. You're ready!